WISCONSIN TRIVIA

WISCONSIN TRIVIA

COMPILED BY
KRISTIN VISSER

Rutledge Hill Press
Nashville, Tennessee

Published by Rutledge Hill Press, Inc.
211 Seventh Avenue North
Nashville, Tennessee 37219

Typography by D&T/Bailey, Nashville, Tennessee

Library of Congress Cataloging-in-Publication Data

Visser, Kristin, 1949–
  Wisconsin trivia / compiled by Kristin Visser.
    p.   cm.
  ISBN 1-55853-297-8 : $5.95
  1. Wisconsin—Miscellanea.   I. Title.
F581.5V57   1994
877.5'0078—dc20   94-20370
                                                                    CIP

Printed in the United States of America
2 3 4 5 6 7—98 97 96 95 94

PREFACE

Compiling nearly 1,300 trivia questions about Wisconsin reminded me what a wonderful and diverse state it is. Wisconsin's past and present are full of adventure and exploration, political intrigue, great discoveries in science and technology, fascinating natural wonders, and equally fascinating people.

With so much to draw on, it was easy to find interesting tidbits about historic figures such as Robert La Follette and Douglas MacArthur, about world-record fish and world-class works of art and literature, about festivals and historic events, Indian tribes and European settlers, our diverse industries and our lovely landscape, and about the famous personalities who grew up here or made the state their home. I ran out of space long before I ran out of ideas and questions.

I hope long-time residents and newcomers alike will find *Wisconsin Trivia* informative, challenging, and fun.

Kristin Visser

To
Jerry Minnich
For his help and encouragement

TABLE OF CONTENTS

GEOGRAPHY

C H A P T E R   O N E

Q. Which of the Apostle Islands is the largest?

A. Madeline.

◆

Q. In 1850, what proportion of Wisconsin residents were immigrants from foreign countries?

A. One-third.

◆

Q. Where is the oldest military academy in Wisconsin?

A. Delafield (St. John's Military Academy).

◆

Q. During World War I, of what was DuPont's Barksdale Works on the shore of Chequamegon Bay the world's largest producer?

A. Dynamite.

◆

Q. Where was Wisconsin's first school for the deaf?

A. In the Walworth County village of Delavan.

Q. Where was Wisconsin's first nuclear power plant?

A. Genoa (on the Mississippi River).

----◆----

Q. Where is the world's largest six-pack?

A. At the Heileman Brewery in La Crosse.

----◆----

Q. How did the Bad River get its name?

A. French fur traders called it "mauvaise" (bad) because it was difficult to navigate.

----◆----

Q. What canal was built to shorten the time required to travel from Milwaukee to Green Bay by ship?

A. The Sturgeon Bay Ship Canal.

----◆----

Q. How long is the Wisconsin River?

A. 430 miles.

----◆----

Q. What product from the Bayfield area helped build cities as far east as New York and Boston?

A. Sandstone (called brownstone for its distinctive color).

----◆----

Q. Where is the northernmost post office in Wisconsin?

A. Cornucopia (54827), on the Bayfield Peninsula.

Q. Where is the only operating mine in Wisconsin?

A. Ladysmith.

Q. What Wisconsin town calls itself "Home of the Hamburger"?

A. Seymour.

Q. Where is the world's only oval track dogsled race?

A. Eagle River (held during Klondike Days in February).

Q. What does *Kenosha* mean?

A. It is Potawatomi for "pike" or "pickerel."

Q. Where is Gen. Dwight Eisenhower's World War II private railcar?

A. At the National Railroad Museum in Green Bay.

Q. What was Wisconsin's earliest lead mine?

A. The St. John mine in Potosi (1827; it was worked by Indians even earlier).

Q. How many islands are in the Apostle group?

A. Twenty-two.

Q. Where was Wisconsin's first iron smelter situated?

A. Mayville (producing from 1849 until 1928).

——◆——

Q. Which Wisconsin community is a popular destination for Swiss tourists?

A. New Glarus (founded in 1845 by Swiss immigrants).

——◆——

Q. How much did land in downtown Milwaukee sell for at the height of the 1830s' land boom?

A. $4,000 an acre.

——◆——

Q. What did the National Geographic Society get from UW-Madison cartographer Arthur Robinson in 1988?

A. Its new world map.

——◆——

Q. According to one legend, where is Paul Bunyan buried?

A. Under Rib Mountain at Wausau.

——◆——

Q. Where is the Loon Capital of the World?

A. Mercer.

——◆——

Q. How many national forests are in Wisconsin?

A. Two (Nicolet and Chequamegon).

Q. What Wisconsin city is the home of the Liars Club?

A. Burlington.

------◆------

Q. What state provided the most U.S.-born immigrants to Wisconsin in the 1840s?

A. New York.

------◆------

Q. From its source to its mouth, how far does the Wisconsin River drop in altitude?

A. 1,071 feet (from Lac Vieux Desert to Prairie du Chien).

------◆------

Q. How many dams are on the Wisconsin River?

A. Forty-seven (twenty-one reservoir and twenty-six hydro-electric).

------◆------

Q. Which Wisconsin county produces the most corn?

A. Dane.

------◆------

Q. Where was the nation's first large-scale soil and water conservation project?

A. The Coon Creek Watershed (west of La Crosse), chosen in 1933.

------◆------

Q. Where did Adele Brice see the Virgin Mary in 1858?

A. Champion (then called Robinsonville) in Brown County.

Q. Why is Oshkosh called "the Sawdust City"?

A. Because of the many sawmills and wood products manufacturers in the city in the mid- to late-1800s.

———◆———

Q. Where was Wisconsin's first consolidated school district formed in 1903?

A. Port Wing.

———◆———

Q. What is the Baraboo Range?

A. One of the world's most ancient mountain ranges (worn down over hundreds of millions of years of erosion).

———◆———

Q. Forests cover what percentage of the state?

A. Almost forty-five percent.

———◆———

Q. In what Wisconsin community's name is every other letter an "o"?

A. Oconomowoc.

———◆———

Q. Where is the Wisconsin Conservation Hall of Fame?

A. On the campus of UW-Stevens Point.

———◆———

Q. What is the highest waterfall in Wisconsin?

A. Big Manitou Falls (165 feet).

Q. Where was Wisconsin's first prison built in 1851?

A. Waupun.

Q. What is the total area, in acres, of Wisconsin?

A. 35.8 million.

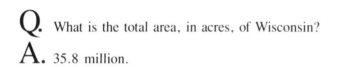

Q. Where is the Toilet Paper Capital of the World?

A. Green Bay.

Q. What was the route of the first cross-Wisconsin railroad, completed in 1857?

A. Milwaukee to Prairie du Chien.

Q. Where was "Chair City" in the 1890s?

A. Sheboygan.

Q. What is the largest lake in Wisconsin?

A. Lake Winnebago (covers 215 square miles).

Q. How did Governor Lee Sherman Dreyfus refer to Madison?

A. He called it "Thirty-six square miles surrounded by reality."

Q. What town is situated at the geographic center of Wisconsin?

A. Pittsville.

Q. What two places claim to be "the Muskie Capital of the World"?

A. Hayward and Boulder Junction.

Q. What county is known as the "bellwether" county for voting for winners in elections?

A. Trempealeau.

Q. What city is the home of Jockey shorts?

A. Kenosha.

———◆———

Q. For what was the city of Ashland named?

A. Henry Clay's Kentucky plantation.

———◆———

Q. What is the smallest Wisconsin county?

A. Ozaukee (232 square miles).

———◆———

Q. What state supplied the lumber for the first Wisconsin territorial Capitol of 1836?

A. Pennsylvania.

Q. What is the total area, in square miles, of Wisconsin?

A. 56,066.

———◆———

Q. Where was the last manned lighthouse on the Great Lakes?

A. Sherwood Point (just south of Sturgeon Bay).

———◆———

Q. Where is the longest undammed stretch of river in the Midwest?

A. Ninety-two miles of the lower Wisconsin River from Prairie du Sac to Prairie du Chien.

———◆———

Q. Where was the ice cream sundae invented?

A. Two Rivers.

———◆———

Q. Where is the northernmost Confederate cemetery?

A. Forest Hill in Madison.

———◆———

Q. Where is the geographic center of the northern half of the western hemisphere (45 degrees north latitude, 90 degrees longitude)?

A. In a farm field near Poniatowski, in Marathon County.

———◆———

Q. What Wisconsin village declared war and threatened to secede from the state after being left off the official 1967 highway map?

A. Winneconne.

Q. During what event does Oshkosh's Wittman Field become the world's busiest airport?

A. The annual Experimental Aircraft Association fly-in.

◆

Q. In which Wisconsin community have the most UFOs been spotted?

A. Belleville (more than a dozen).

◆

Q. How many counties are in Wisconsin?

A. Seventy-two.

◆

Q. Who lives at Holy Hill?

A. A group of discalced Carmelite friars.

◆

Q. What states border Wisconsin?

A. Minnesota, Iowa, Illinois, and Michigan.

◆

Q. On what river is Big Manitou Falls?

A. The Black.

◆

Q. How does Wisconsin rank in size among all states?

A. Twenty-sixth.

Q. In what park are the major historic buildings of Green Bay gathered in one spot?

A. Heritage Hill State Park.

Q. Where are the world's largest ore docks?

A. Superior.

Q. What are the real names of "Point," "Fort," "Rapids," and "Tosa"?

A. Stevens Point, Fort Atkinson, Wisconsin Rapids, and Wauwatosa, respectively.

Q. Where is Rosemary Kennedy, sister of John F. Kennedy?

A. At St. Coletta's School in Jefferson.

Q. What lake never gives up her dead?

A. Lake Superior.

Q. Where is mail-order giant Lands' End?

A. Dodgeville.

Q. What Wisconsin river has the nation's highest density of paper mills?

A. The Fox (between Appleton and Green Bay).

Q. Where do you buy Rippin' Good Cookies fresh from the oven?

A. Ripon.

———◆———

Q. What Racine company has become the generic name for garbage disposals?

A. In-sink-erator.

———◆———

Q. Where is the largest four-faced clock in the world?

A. On the tower of the Allen Bradley Company in Milwaukee.

———◆———

Q. In which county are the Eau Claire Dells?

A. Marathon.

———◆———

Q. The 1825 opening of what eastern U.S. waterway made it easier for goods and people to move between Wisconsin and the East?

A. The Erie Canal.

———◆———

Q. How many lakes are in Wisconsin?

A. About 15,000.

———◆———

Q. What is the largest county in Wisconsin?

A. Marathon (1,545.1 square miles).

Q. Where is the "Shipbuilding Capital of the Great Lakes"?

A. Sturgeon Bay.

Q. What is Wisconsin's most populous county?

A. Milwaukee (970,000 residents as of 1993).

Q. Where are Wisconsin's highest sand dunes?

A. Whitefish Dunes State Park (Door County).

Q. How many Indian reservations does Wisconsin have?

A. Eleven.

Q. What geologic formation underlies northeast Wisconsin, from Door County south to Fond du Lac?

A. The Niagara Escarpment.

Q. How many miles of roads does Wisconsin have?

A. 111,000.

Q. For what purpose was Delavan founded in 1836?

A. As a Baptist temperance community.

Q. Where is the state's largest celebration of Norwegian Independence Day?

A. Stoughton.

———◆———

Q. How did Oshkosh get its name?

A. From the Menominee's Chief Oshkosh.

———◆———

Q. What is unique about the Dane County community of Waunakee?

A. It's the only town with that name in the world.

———◆———

Q. Which Wisconsin county has the most lakes?

A. Vilas.

———◆———

Q. Where did FBI agents engage in a shootout with John Dillinger in April 1934?

A. Little Bohemia resort near Manitowish Waters.

———◆———

Q. Where did the nickname Badger State originate?

A. Miners in southwest Wisconsin were called badgers because they burrowed into the hills.

———◆———

Q. Where is Wisconsin's largest concentration of effigy mounds?

A. More than 1,000 have been counted in the Madison area.

Q. Where was the only Wisconsin battle of the War of 1812 fought?

A. Prairie du Chien.

Q. What is the highest point in Wisconsin?

A. Timm's Hill in Price County (1951.8 feet above sea level).

Q. What southern Wisconsin resort community was called the Newport of the West in the late nineteenth century?

A. Lake Geneva.

Q. What is unique about Reedsburg's location?

A. It is the only Wisconsin community that is on the 90th parallel of longitude.

Q. Where was the world's first hydroelectric generating plant opened in 1882?

A. Appleton.

Q. For what baked good is Racine famous?

A. Danish kringle.

Q. Who founded Janesville in 1836?

A. Henry Janes.

Q. How long is the Sturgeon Bay Ship Canal?

A. 7,400 feet.

Q. What city was created through the consolidation of Juneau-town, Kilbourntown, and Walker's Point?

A. Milwaukee.

Q. What three rivers flow through Milwaukee?

A. The Kinnickinnic, the Menomonee, and the Milwaukee.

Q. What does *Milwaukee* mean in the Potawatomi language?

A. "Gathering place by the waters."

Q. Where does Jimmy the Groundhog come out to look for his shadow every February 2?

A. Sun Prairie.

Q. What northern Wisconsin community is the birthplace of the snowmobile?

A. Sayner.

Q. What was the route of Wisconsin's first railroad, opened in 1851?

A. It ran ten miles from Milwaukee to Waukesha.

Q. Where did gangster Al Capone have a northwoods retreat?

A. At Couderay, in Sawyer County.

———◆———

Q. Which Indian tribes live in Wisconsin?

A. The Chippewa, Potawatomi, Menominee, Stockbridge-Munsee, Oneida, and Winnebago.

———◆———

Q. What Wisconsin county is the center of the nation's largest ginseng growing industry?

A. Marathon.

———◆———

Q. Where did Al Capone's brother Ralph live and operate a tavern for decades until his death in 1974?

A. Mercer.

———◆———

Q. Where is the Dairy Shrine?

A. Fort Atkinson.

———◆———

Q. Where did John Muir's family settle when they emigrated from Scotland to Wisconsin?

A. A farm just north of Portage.

———◆———

Q. Where is the nation's largest Icelandic settlement?

A. Washington Island.

Q. Where was U.S. Supreme Court Chief Justice William Rehnquist born?

A. Milwaukee.

Q. Who are the oldest continuous residents of Wisconsin?

A. The Menominee, who have been in the area for 5,000 years.

Q. What was the purpose of the Portage Canal?

A. To connect the Fox and Wisconsin rivers for navigation.

Q. Where is the nation's largest Army Reserve training and mobilization center?

A. Fort McCoy (near Sparta).

Q. What is Wisconsin's "Great Wall of China"?

A. A wall displaying hundreds of bathroom fixtures at the Kohler Design Center in Kohler.

Q. Where have archaeologists found the earliest evidence of human habitation in Wisconsin?

A. Near Kenosha.

Q. What is Wisconsin's least populous county?

A. Menominee (under 4,000 residents in 1993).

Q. Where did teacher Bernard Cigrand lead the first observance of Flag Day in 1885?

A. At Stony Hill School in Waubeka.

Q. Where does the *Karfi* ferry go?

A. From Jackson Harbor on Washington Island to Rock Island.

Q. Where were the first two Norwegian settlements in Wisconsin?

A. At Jefferson Prairie and Rock Prairie (in present-day Rock County).

Q. What document guarantees freedom of navigation on Wisconsin waters?

A. The Northwest Ordinance of 1787.

Q. Where was the nation's first electric power generating station owned by a cooperative?

A. Chippewa Falls.

Q. Dawn Manor on Lake Delton is the sole survivor of what ill-fated boomtown?

A. Newport.

Q. When was Wisconsin's first Rustic Road designated?

A. September 27, 1975 (Rustic Road One, near Rib Lake).

Q. Where is the Wisconsin State Championship Cherry Pit Spit held?

A. Fish Creek.

Q. From what point do all Wisconsin public land surveys begin?

A. From a mound built (now demolished) by surveyors in 1831 on the Illinois-Wisconsin border near Hazel Green.

Q. Where is the last historic covered bridge in Wisconsin?

A. Just outside Cedarburg.

Q. Into what two principal drainage areas does all water in Wisconsin flow?

A. The Mississippi River and Great Lakes watersheds.

Q. Before 1931, what was the name of Wisconsin Dells?

A. Kilbourn City.

Q. Where was the Saratoga of the West in the late nineteenth century?

A. Waukesha.

Q. What beverage was sold under such names as Bethesda, Hygia, Vesta, Lethesn, Arcadian, Fountain, Clysmic, Glenn, Tonyawatha, and Vita?

A. Water from Wisconsin springs.

Q. Where is the Midwest's most popular rock climbing spot?

A. Devil's Lake State Park in Sauk County.

Q. Where is the Mid-Continent Railway Museum?

A. North Freedom.

Q. What is the surface area of Lake Michigan?

A. 22,300 square miles.

Q. In 1980, Fort McCoy was used as a processing site for what group of immigrants?

A. Cubans who arrived during the Mariel boatlift.

Q. Where was historian Frederick Jackson Turner born in 1861?

A. Portage.

Q. Before the federal government sold the site for Potawatomi State Park in Door County to the state, for what use was the land being considered?

A. A naval training station.

Q. Dyckesville, Namur, and Brussels were settled by what group of immigrants?

A. Belgians.

Q. What is the largest island in Wisconsin?

A. Washington Island (thirty-six square miles).

Q. Which two Indian tribes were moved to Wisconsin from the East in the 1830s to make room for white settlement?

A. The Stockbridge-Munsee and the Oneidas.

Q. Where is Wisconsin's oldest lighthouse (built in 1836)?

A. Rock Island.

Q. What religious group founded the village of Ephraim in 1853?

A. Moravians from Norway.

Q. How did Sister Bay get its name?

A. From the two islands just offshore.

Q. Where in Door County do you find Eagle Bluff, Sven's Bluff, and Norway Bluff?

A. Peninsula State Park.

Q. What is the population of Wisconsin?

A. 5,038,000 (as of 1993).

Q. Who is buried in the golf course at Peninsula State Park?

A. Potawatomi chief Simon Kahquados (buried there in 1931).

Q. For whom is Marinette named?

A. For Marinette, granddaughter of a Chippewa chief who ran a store in the community from the early 1820s until 1865.

Q. What used to occupy the site of Newport State Park in Door County?

A. The village of Newport (a timber shipping port in the 1870s).

Q. Where is Death's Door?

A. At the tip of the Door Peninsula between the mainland and Washington Island.

Q. What is the route of the Lake Michigan car ferry?

A. From Manitowoc to Ludington, Michigan.

Q. What 1959 event connected Wisconsin Great Lakes ports with the Atlantic Ocean?

A. The opening of the St. Lawrence Seaway.

Q. Where is the only surviving example of the Great Lakes ship called a "whaleback"?

A. Superior.

Q. Where is Wisconsin's only cooperage museum?

A. Bayfield.

Q. What is "the most Danish City in America"?

A. Racine.

Q. Where can you tour a World War II submarine?

A. At the Manitowoc Maritime Museum.

Q. Where is the largest grandfather clock in Wisconsin?

A. Outside the headquarters of Svaboda Industries in Kewaunee.

Q. What is Sturgeon Bay's largest industry?

A. Shipbuilding, repair, and maintenance.

Q. What is Bjorklunden Chapel near Bailey's Harbor a copy of?

A. A Norwegian "stavekirke" (wooden church).

Q. What is stovewood construction, as practiced by many nineteenth-century German immigrants?

A. Stove-length pieces of wood are stacked and mortared together so that the ends create the inner and outer walls of a building.

Q. What exclusive resort was originally built as housing and recreation facilities for factory workers?

A. The American Club in Kohler.

———◆———

Q. For what glacial landforms are the Kettle Moraines named?

A. Kettles are small pothole lakes; moraines are gravelly hills deposited at the leading edge of a glacier.

———◆———

Q. What put the Wade House Stagecoach Inn in Greenbush out of business?

A. The railroad bypassed Greenbush in 1860.

———◆———

Q. Where were most of the carriages on view in the Jung Carriage Museum in Greenbush built?

A. At the Jacob Jung Carriage Factory in Sheboygan.

———◆———

Q. What did German Catholic immigrants led by Fr. Ambrose Oschwald begin at St. Nazianz in 1854?

A. A communal religious settlement that lasted until 1873.

———◆———

Q. What Wisconsin community was known as "the Clipper City" for its boatyards?

A. Manitowoc.

———◆———

Q. How high above sea level is the surface of Lake Michigan?

A. 531 feet.

Q. What is Wisconsin's only car ferry across the Mississippi?

A. The Cassville ferry (carries cars to Iowa every summer).

———◆———

Q. Where is the Tubing Capital of the World?

A. Somerset on the Apple River.

———◆———

Q. Where is Wisconsin's Vietnam Veterans' Memorial Park?

A. Neillsville.

———◆———

Q. Where does Susie the duck live?

A. In Lodi.

———◆———

Q. Rock Island State Park is part of what group of islands?

A. The Grand Traverse Islands (Rock, Detroit, Pilot, Plum, and Fish islands).

———◆———

Q. Where are the Lumberjack World Championships held every July?

A. Hayward.

———◆———

Q. What is the deepest point of Lake Michigan?

A. 923 feet.

Q. Where is Wisconsin's largest mountain bike race, the Chequamegon Fat Tire Festival Race, held every September?

A. Cable.

◆

Q. Where is Claire, at 16½ feet high the world's largest loon?

A. Mercer.

◆

Q. In what museum is there a life-size wood carving of the Last Supper?

A. The Museum of Woodcarving in Shell Lake.

◆

Q. Where is Wisconsin's only working covered bridge, opened in 1991?

A. At Smith Falls Campground (near Park Falls in the Chequamegon National Forest).

◆

Q. What community puts on the annual Logjam Festival?

A. Wausau.

◆

Q. Which two Wisconsin counties have no incorporated communities?

A. Florence and Menominee.

◆

Q. Where do the World Snowmobile Racing Championships take place every January?

A. Eagle River.

Q. What central Wisconsin community was called "the Gateway to the Pineries"?

A. Stevens Point.

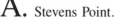

Q. In which municipal park can you find pieces of the Great Wall of China and stones from the Damascus Road?

A. Pioneer Park in Clintonville.

Q. Where is Wisconsin's only solar-powered downtown?

A. Soldiers Grove.

Q. Where do Wisconsin mustard lovers congregate?

A. At the Mt. Horeb Mustard Museum.

Q. What kind of tower does Tower Hill State Park preserve?

A. A shot tower for making lead shot by dropping molten lead 120 feet into a pool.

Q. Where is Norway's "stavekirke" (wooden church) building from the 1893 Chicago World's Fair?

A. Little Norway in Mt. Horeb.

Q. Where are the U.S. Watermelon Seed-spitting and Speed-eating Championships held?

A. Pardeeville.

Q. What is Wisconsin's first state park?

A. Interstate (created in 1900).

------◆------

Q. What celebration culminates with the Parade of Roasts through downtown Minocqua?

A. Beef-a-Rama.

------◆------

Q. In what foreign countries does Wisconsin have state employees?

A. It has international trade representatives in Hong Kong, Japan, Germany, South Korea, Canada, and Mexico.

------◆------

Q. What is the surface area of Lake Superior?

A. 31,700 square miles.

------◆------

Q. What is the Vesterheim Genealogical Center in Madison?

A. The nation's largest repository of information about Norwegian immigration to the United States.

------◆------

Q. How many miles of trout streams are in Wisconsin?

A. 9,560.

------◆------

Q. How many lakes of more than fifty acres are in Wisconsin?

A. 15,000.

Q. What Wisconsin town calls itself the "Rope Jumping Capital of the World"?

A. Bloomer.

Q. For how many miles does the Mississippi River form the western border of Wisconsin?

A. 190.

Q. Where is the Heart of the North Rodeo held every July?

A. Spooner.

Q. What is the largest Indian reservation in Wisconsin?

A. The Menominee Reservation (234,900 acres).

Q. How many miles of Great Lakes shoreline are within Wisconsin?

A. 860.

Q. If Portage is the county seat of Columbia County, what is the county seat of Portage County?

A. Stevens Point.

Q. Why is the Eagle River chain of lakes notable?

A. Its twenty-eight lakes form the world's longest connected chain.

Q. Where is the National Freshwater Fishing Hall of Fame?

A. Hayward.

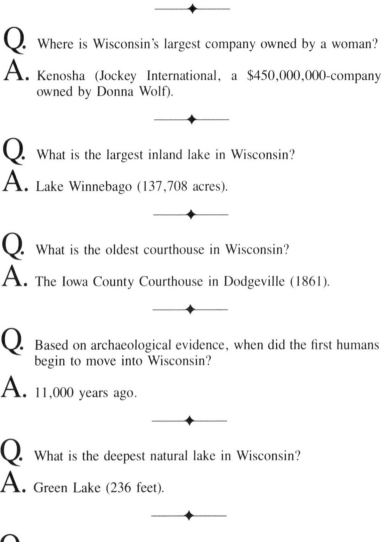

Q. Where is Wisconsin's largest company owned by a woman?

A. Kenosha (Jockey International, a $450,000,000-company owned by Donna Wolf).

Q. What is the largest inland lake in Wisconsin?

A. Lake Winnebago (137,708 acres).

Q. What is the oldest courthouse in Wisconsin?

A. The Iowa County Courthouse in Dodgeville (1861).

Q. Based on archaeological evidence, when did the first humans begin to move into Wisconsin?

A. 11,000 years ago.

Q. What is the deepest natural lake in Wisconsin?

A. Green Lake (236 feet).

Q. What is the largest Wisconsin state park?

A. Devil's Lake (just under 8,800 acres).

Q. Where is the annual Great Black River Rubber Duck Race, with 4,000 rubber ducks, held?

A. Medford.

Q. Where is the U.S. International Snow Sculpting Championship held every January?

A. Milwaukee.

Q. Which Wisconsin county has the fewest lakes?

A. Crawford.

Q. What does the Ice Age Trail follow across Wisconsin?

A. The southernmost edge of the glacier's last advance.

Q. What route did French explorers discover in 1680 to speed travel from Lake Superior south?

A. The Brule and St. Croix rivers (with a short portage between) as a route south to the Mississippi.

Q. How long has a ferry been operating on the Wisconsin River at Merrimac?

A. Since 1844.

Q. What Wisconsin county was the first in the United States to adopt rural zoning regulations?

A. Oneida (1933).

Q. How long is the Door County Peninsula?

A. Seventy miles.

Q. Where was the 1928 summer White House?

A. Superior Central High School (while Calvin Coolidge visited northern Wisconsin).

Q. When did Wisconsin's first stretch of interstate highway open?

A. 1958, in Waukesha County.

Q. How many years did it take Bernard Cigrand to get the federal government to declare a national observance for Flag Day?

A. Thirty-one.

Q. If Dodgeville is the county seat of Iowa County, what is the county seat of Dodge County?

A. Juneau.

Q. What is the easternmost point in Wisconsin?

A. The eastern shore of Rock Island, off the coast of Door County.

Q. What is Wisconsin's most common lake name?

A. Mud Lake (at least 115 lakes in the state have this name).

Q. Which Wisconsin Indian tribe has the most reservations?

A. The Chippewa (six).

———◆———

Q. What was Rock Island before the state purchased it for a park?

A. The estate of Icelandic inventor Chester Thordarson.

———◆———

Q. What is the deepest point in Lake Superior?

A. 1,330 feet.

———◆———

Q. What was the first road to cross Wisconsin?

A. The Military Road, built in 1835–36 from Prairie du Chien to Green Bay via Portage.

———◆———

Q. How many miles of shoreline does Door County have?

A. 250 (more than any other county in the United States).

———◆———

Q. Where was the nation's first school forest (used for nature study and as a nature preserve)?

A. Laona, in Forest County (1928).

———◆———

Q. How many churches have been built on the site of Holy Hill near Milwaukee?

A. Three (1860, 1880, and the present one, dedicated in 1931).

ENTERTAINMENT

C H A P T E R   T W O

Q. Kenosha's Harmony Hall is the national headquarters for what organization?

A. The Society for the Preservation and Encouragement of Barbershop Singing in America.

———◆———

Q. In what 1984 film did space alien Jeff Bridges land in Wisconsin?

A. *Starman.*

———◆———

Q. What Manitowoc band is known for its "polka-rap," with such songs as a polka "Born to Be Wild" and the "Pump It Up Polka"?

A. The Happy Schnapps Combo.

———◆———

Q. Who is the most famous graduate of UW-Superior?

A. Arnold Schwarzenegger.

———◆———

Q. What is "fifth quarter" at a UW-Madison home football game?

A. A half-hour post-game show by the UW Marching Band.

Q. Where was Annie Hall's hometown?

A. Chippewa Falls.

Q. Where was the rock band BoDeans organized?

A. Waukesha.

Q. Under what name do Milwaukee keyboardist Connie Grauer and drummer Kim Zick perform?

A. Mrs. Fun.

Q. What Reedsburg native's cartoons depicting his boyhood and other simple pleasures made him popular with readers of the *St. Louis Globe-Democrat* and *New York Herald Tribune*?

A. Clare Briggs (born in 1875).

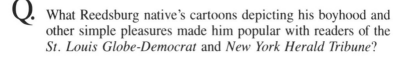

Q. Who created the award-winning comic book series *Nexus*?

A. Madison writer Mike Baron and former Madison resident Steve Rude.

Q. Who are the Wisconsin members of the Grammy-winning rap group Arrested Development?

A. Speech (Milwaukee) and Aerle Taree Jones (Madison).

Q. Which star of "Saturday Night Live" is from Wisconsin?

A. Chris Farley (Maple Bluff).

Q. What Madison-based Norwegian trio was famous for such tunes as "There's No Norwegians in Dickeyville" and "The Beach at Waunakee"?

A. The Goose Island Ramblers.

—◆—

Q. Where was bandleader Mitchell Ayres born in 1910?

A. Milwaukee.

—◆—

Q. What Madison band known for Latin music got its start at a 1981 party for Chilean students?

A. Sotovento.

—◆—

Q. Where did singer Otis Redding die?

A. Madison's Lake Monona (in a plane crash in 1967).

—◆—

Q. Where was singer Glenn Yarborough born in 1930?

A. Milwaukee.

—◆—

Q. As head of the Federal Communications Commission, what Milwaukee native labeled television a "vast wasteland"?

A. Newton Minow.

—◆—

Q. According to the song "The Big Red Badgers Go to Pasadena," what powered the 1994 Badger Rose Bowl team?

A. Cheese.

Q. In what TV series did Milwaukee Brewers announcer Bob Uecker star?

A. "Mr. Belvedere."

Q. Where did Jill Eikenberry, star of TV's "L.A. Law," attend high school?

A. Madison West.

Q. Who is the only U.S. senator who owns a professional basketball team?

A. Wisconsin Senator Herb Kohl (owns the Milwaukee Bucks).

Q. What actress do the Zucker brothers always use in their movies?

A. Their mother, Shorewood actress Charlotte Zucker.

Q. Before the 1994 Rose Bowl, Universal Studios in Hollywood offered free admission to Badger fans who did what?

A. Brought either a live badger or a Badger football player with them.

Q. What Manitowoc rock musician played with British rocker Dave Mason and wrote the hit song "We Just Disagree"?

A. Jim Krueger.

Q. Where is Wisconsin's largest Renaissance Faire held every summer?

A. Bristol.

Q. Who did Fond du Lac honor in 1990 by making him an honorary cheesehead and creating a forty-five-pound cheddar cheese bust in his likeness?

A. *Chicago Tribune* columnist Mike Royko.

Q. What Milwaukee native won Grammys in 1978 and 1979 for jazz singing?

A. Al Jarreau.

Q. Under what name did Appleton resident Ehrich Weiss become famous?

A. Harry Houdini.

Q. Where did psychic Jeane Dixon grow up?

A. Medford.

Q. What Racine vocalist was a regular on the "Sing Along with Mitch" TV variety show and later became one of the first African-American women to host her own TV show?

A. Barbara McNair.

Q. What is the oldest continually operating radio station in the world?

A. WHA radio in Madison, broadcasting since 1917.

Q. Who starred in the 1957 film *All Mine to Give*, about a family in the Wisconsin wilderness?

A. Glynis Johns and Cameron Mitchell.

Q. Under what name has Milwaukee native Jerry Silberman gained fame?

A. Gene Wilder.

———◆———

Q. When did "America's Dairyland" first appear on Wisconsin license plates?

A. 1940.

———◆———

Q. What actress, nominated for Best Supporting Actress for her role in *Working Girl*, graduated from UW-Madison in 1984?

A. Joan Cusack.

———◆———

Q. What Wisconsin company publishes Little Golden Books?

A. Western Publishing (Racine).

———◆———

Q. Where was actor Tom Hulce, who gained fame in the film *Amadeus*, born?

A. Whitewater.

———◆———

Q. What two Ripon College students became acting superstars?

A. Spencer Tracy and Harrison Ford.

———◆———

Q. What Token Creek composer won the 1987 Pulitzer Prize for composition?

A. John Harbison.

Q. What Door County restaurant is known for its sod roof, complete with grazing goats?

A. Al Johnson's Swedish Restaurant.

Q. What Appleton native's big film break came in the 1986 movie *Platoon*?

A. Willem Dafoe.

Q. What Kenosha native capped a fifty-year radio, TV, and film career with a Best Supporting Actor Oscar for the movie *Cocoon*?

A. Don Ameche.

Q. Where was actor and singer Dennis Morgan born?

A. Prentice (1910).

Q. Where was film director Joseph Losey born?

A. La Crosse.

———◆———

Q. What Madison comedy troupe was founded by Jerry and David Zucker and Jim Abrahams?

A. Kentucky Fried Theater.

———◆———

Q. What project brought Rodney Dangerfield and Sally Kellerman to the UW-Madison campus in 1986?

A. Filming the movie *Back to School*.

Q. Where does the CBS soap opera "The Young and the Restless" take place?

A. Genoa City, Wisconsin.

Q. What is the hometown of jazz great Bunny Berigan?

A. Fox Lake.

Q. When did public television station WHA-TV go on the air?

A. 1954.

Q. What Milwaukee native made millions with a publishing empire that included *TV Guide*?

A. Walter Annenberg, Jr.

Q. What Milwaukee theater company is known for its avant garde works and its ties with theaters in Holland?

A. Theater X.

Q. What were actors Nick Nolte and Julia Roberts doing in the Madison area in the fall of 1993?

A. Filming the movie *I Love Trouble*.

Q. Where was actor, director, and writer Orson Welles born in 1915?

A. Kenosha.

Q. Which of Edgerton author Sterling North's books were made into films by Disney?

A. *Rascal* and *So Dear to My Heart*.

◆

Q. On what notorious Wisconsin murderer was the Anthony Perkins character in the movie *Psycho* based?

A. Ed Gein.

◆

Q. The uncle of what well-known movie star donated the money to complete the Howard Young Medical Center in Woodruff?

A. Elizabeth Taylor.

◆

Q. Who is Wisconsin's only Miss America?

A. Terry Anne Meeuwsen of DePere (1973).

◆

Q. The tune that became "On, Wisconsin" was written with the hope that what football team would adopt it?

A. University of Minnesota.

◆

Q. What Wisconsin community was used for the filming of the movie version of Ernest Hemingway's *Adventures of a Young Man*?

A. The Iron County community of Saxon.

◆

Q. What Milwaukee native twice won the Academy Award for best actor?

A. Spencer Tracy.

Q. Who led Perry Como's orchestra on his radio and TV shows?

A. Mitchell Ayres.

Q. What major collection of film materials is housed at the UW-Madison Center for Theater Research?

A. The United Artists collection of corporate records, films, publicity materials, and photographs.

Q. What was the Sheboygan-based Chordettes' big 1954 hit?

A. "Mr. Sandman."

Q. What internationally known bassist teaches at UW-Madison?

A. Richard Davis.

Q. Who was Spencer Tracy's best friend while growing up in Milwaukee?

A. Pat O'Brien, who later starred in such movies as *Knute Rockne—All American*.

Q. Where was Liberace born?

A. West Allis (1919).

Q. What Mineral Point native became famous as the host of TV's "College Bowl" and "Password"?

A. Allen Ludden.

Q. What TV show made Lodi native Tom Wopat a star?

A. "The Dukes of Hazzard."

Q. What Kenosha native starred in "Hill Street Blues"?

A. Dan Travanti.

Q. What nationally known jazz pianist lives in Madison?

A. Ben Sidran.

Q. What advertising sensation did Oscar Mayer, headquartered in Madison, introduce in 1936?

A. The Wienermobile (driven by Little Oscar, the midget chef).

Q. Who hosted the Milwaukee public television show "Hatha Yoga" that began in 1970 and ran for more than twenty years?

A. Kathleen Hitchcock.

Q. Where was actress Tyne Daly born?

A. Madison.

Q. What hard rock band got its start in the National Honor Society talent show at Milwaukee's Rufus King High School?

A. The Violent Femmes.

Q. When did the Ringling Brothers put on their first circus performance?

A. In 1884 (in Baraboo).

———◆———

Q. What stage name did Liberace use for a time in the late 1930s?

A. Walter Busterkeys.

———◆———

Q. What invention by Waukesha native and musician Les Paul laid the foundation for rock-and-roll?

A. The electric guitar.

———◆———

Q. What Milwaukee-born blues guitarist and band leader got his start while a student at UW-Madison?

A. Steve Miller.

———◆———

Q. Which Milwaukee big band leader's biggest hit was "Woodchopper's Ball"?

A. Woody Herman.

———◆———

Q. What Wisconsin-born musician wrote the Tennessee state song?

A. Pee Wee King ("The Tennessee Waltz").

———◆———

Q. Who composed "On, Wisconsin"?

A. William Purdy (music) and UW alumnus Carl Beck (lyrics).

Q. Who wrote the wedding favorites "I Love You Truly" and "O Promise Me"?

A. Carrie Jacobs Bond of Janesville.

Q. TSR, Inc. of Lake Geneva, founded in 1973, produces and markets what game?

A. Dungeons and Dragons.

Q. Where is the world's largest collection of neon advertising signs?

A. In the Antigo office of Dean Blazek (president of Northern Advertising).

Q. What Racine native twice won the Academy Award for best actor?

A. Frederic March.

Q. Where is the world's largest carousel?

A. At The House on the Rock near Spring Green.

Q. Who was the Wisconsin-born member of the Talking Heads?

A. Jerry Harrison.

Q. What happened after a concert at Alpine Valley on August 28, 1990?

A. Guitarist Stevie Ray Vaughn was killed in a helicopter crash.

Q. Where is the world's largest circus parade, the Great Circus Parade, held every July?

A. Milwaukee.

Q. Where was the 1994 Disney release *Iron Will* shot?

A. In Superior, Oliver, Brule River State Forest, and Hoodoo Lake (along with Minnesota locations).

Q. At what Wisconsin college did actress Colleen Dewhurst begin her career?

A. Downer College for Young Women.

Q. Racine's Ellen Corby became famous for what role?

A. Grandma Walton in the 1970s TV series "The Waltons."

Q. At what Wisconsin racetrack were portions of the 1969 Paul Newman film *Winning* shot?

A. Road America at Elkhart Lake.

———◆———

Q. What character actress and Milwaukee native had leading roles in such TV shows as "Car 54, Where Are You?", "Diff'rent Strokes," and "Facts of Life"?

A. Charlotte Rae.

———◆———

Q. Who created the comic strip "Gasoline Alley"?

A. Frank King (born in Cashton in 1883).

Q. What is Wisconsin's largest single tourist attraction?

A. The House on the Rock near Spring Green.

Q. What Milwaukee public relations genius resurrected the Great Circus Parade?

A. Ben Barkin.

Q. What did the characters played by Penny Marshall and Cindy Williams in the comedy TV series "Laverne and Shirley" do for a living?

A. Worked at a Milwaukee brewery.

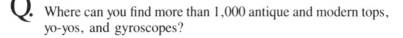

Q. Where was comedian Jackie Mason born?

A. Sheboygan (1934).

Q. Where can you find more than 1,000 antique and modern tops, yo-yos, and gyroscopes?

A. At the Spinning Top Exploratory Museum in Burlington.

Q. What actress and wife of the late John Cassavetes was born in Cambria and attended UW-Madison?

A. Gena Rowlands.

Q. Where did the P. T. Barnum Circus begin?

A. In Delavan, in 1870 (Barnum was a part owner).

Q. German-born actress Uta Hagen was raised in what Wisconsin city?

A. Madison.

Q. Where was actor Michael Cole, who was best known for his role on TV's "Mod Squad," born?

A. Madison (1945).

Q. What Ladysmith native and Vietnam War veteran wrote *Born on the Fourth of July*?

A. Ron Kovic.

Q. Where is the Fireside Restaurant and Playhouse professional dinner theater situated?

A. Fort Atkinson.

Q. Where did comedian George Carlin finally say the famous "seven words" that were prohibited from his TV monologues?

A. At Summerfest in Milwaukee (1972).

Q. Where was film director Nicholas Ray born?

A. Galesburg (1911).

Q. Which of the Righteous Brothers was born in Beaver Dam?

A. Bobby Hatfield.

Q. Where is Krause Publications, the world's largest publisher of hobby magazines, based?

A. Iola.

Q. What was the name of the fictional Wisconsin university in the film *Back to School*?

A. Grand Lakes University.

Q. What nationally broadcast Saturday morning radio talk/quiz show is based at Madison station WHA?

A. "Whad' Ya Know?" with Michael Feldman.

Q. Who built The House on the Rock?

A. Alex Jordan.

Q. Fonzie, Potsie, Ritchie, and Ralph were characters in what Milwaukee-based TV comedy series that ran from 1974 to 1984?

A. "Happy Days."

Q. How much did the Ringling Brothers pay for the Barnum and Bailey circus when they bought it from the widow Bailey in 1907?

A. $410,000.

Q. Where is the Clown Hall of Fame?

A. Delavan.

Q. What well-known trumpeter of the 1930s and early 1940s began his professional career with the Merrill Owen Dance Band of Beaver Dam?

A. Bunny Berigan.

———◆———

Q. When was the jingle "I wish I Was an Oscar Mayer Wiener" first played on the radio?

A. 1963.

———◆———

Q. Who were the original members of the Violent Femmes?

A. Gordon Gano, Brian Ritchie, Victor DeLorenzo.

———◆———

Q. Where is the leather jacket worn by the Fonz on the Wisconsin-based sitcom "Happy Days"?

A. In the Smithsonian Institution in Washington, DC.

———◆———

Q. What 1984 film by Madison-based Yahara Films takes place in Door County?

A. *The Islander.*

———◆———

Q. What is Wisconsin's oldest community theater group?

A. The Haylofters of Burlington.

———◆———

Q. For what TV character is Kenosha actor Al Molinaro best remembered?

A. As Murray the cop on "The Odd Couple."

Q. How have surplus World War II amphibious vehicles found a new life in Wisconsin?

A. As the famous Wisconsin Dells Ducks.

Q. What is the Midwest's only professional theater specializing in American drama?

A. The American Inside Theater in Waukesha.

Q. What Milwaukee-based band, known for its eclectic mixture of blues, jazz, swing, and salsa, lost Robyn Pluer, its lead vocalist, in 1993?

A. Paul Cebar and the Milwaukeeans.

Q. What Bayfield group puts on turn-of-the-century-style productions of plays, musicals, concerts, and lectures outdoors in a big tent?

A. Big Top Chautauqua.

Q. What is America's largest waterpark?

A. Noah's Ark in Wisconsin Dells.

Q. What musical group emulates an actual Wisconsin Civil War band, right down to the antique instruments?

A. The First Brigade Band.

Q. What professional theater company, founded in 1935, is America's oldest professional resident summer theater?

A. Peninsula Players in Fish Creek.

Q. La Crosse native Ford Sterling was chief of what unusual police force?

A. The Keystone Kops.

Q. Who was Les Paul's wife, musical partner, and hometown sweetheart?

A. Mary Ford.

Q. In addition to "On, Wisconsin," what other songs are always heard at UW-Madison athletic events?

A. "Varsity" and "You've Said It All" (also known as the "Bud Song").

Q. Who created the three-ring circus?

A. Delavan circus promoter William Cameron Coup.

Q. Who first "captured" the mythical Rhinelander hodag?

A. Lumberman Gene Shepard (in 1896).

Q. The TV show "Picket Fences" supposedly takes place in what Wisconsin community?

A. Rome.

Q. What famous playboy attended UW-Madison in 1944?

A. Hugh Hefner.

Q. What Milwaukee native was chief writer for Bob Hope and Rudy Vallee in the 1930s, wrote scripts for many of Hope's movies, and co-authored the Broadway hit "L'il Abner"?

A. Melvin Frank.

Q. Who owns the rights to "On, Wisconsin"?

A. Singer Michael Jackson.

Q. What popular 1971 hit movie starred Milwaukeean Tom Laughlin?

A. *Billy Jack.*

Q. What was Wisconsin's first TV station?

A. Milwaukee's WTMJ (December 3, 1947).

———◆———

Q. What 1950s and '60s TV hits did Milwaukee-born scriptwriter Nat Hiken create?

A. "Sgt. Bilko" and "Car 54, Where Are You?".

———◆———

Q. Where did actor Fred MacMurray attend high school and college?

A. Beaver Dam (high school) and Waukesha (Carroll College).

———◆———

Q. What two actors grew up in Milwaukee and starred in the 1946 film *Two Guys from Milwaukee*?

A. Dennis Morgan and Jack Carson.

Q. What UW-Madison grad went on to star with Marilyn Monroe in the classic film *The Seven Year Itch*?

A. Tom Ewell.

Q. Where did Agnes Moorehead teach school before she became an actress?

A. Soldiers Grove (in the mid-1920s).

Q. Who is the director of the UW-Madison marching band?

A. Mike Leckrone.

Q. Milwaukee native Gilda Gray became a star of the Ziegfeld Follies of 1922 and made a triumphal tour of Europe on the basis of what act?

A. The shimmy (her invention became a dance craze).

Q. Who received a Best Supporting Actor award for his role as a Wisconsin lumberjack in the 1936 film version of Edna Ferber's novel *Come and Get It*?

A. Walter Brennen.

Q. In what Wisconsin city did more than two dozen nineteenth-century circuses have their winter quarters?

A. Delavan.

Q. Who were the Milwaukee-born brothers who produced such film classics as *West Side Story*, *Some Like It Hot*, and *Irma La Douce*?

A. Harold, Marvin, and Walter Mirsch.

Q. When Milwaukee native John Freuler began producing films in 1915, whom did he hire to make a series of comedy shorts?

A. Charlie Chaplin.

———◆———

Q. When was "On, Wisconsin" written?

A. 1909.

———◆———

Q. What groundbreaking 1915 film was produced and distributed by Milwaukeean Harry Aitken?

A. *The Birth of a Nation.*

———◆———

Q. Where was the 1991 film *Meet the Applegates* shot?

A. In Appleton and the Fox Valley.

———◆———

Q. What does a hodag eat, according to its captor?

A. "White bulldogs, and those only on Sunday."

———◆———

Q. What was the first animal the Ringling Brothers purchased for their circus menagerie?

A. A hyena (it went on display in 1886).

———◆———

Q. What Madison theater group produces only original plays, with such titles as "The Twisted Love Life of J. Edgar Hoover" and "Sexy Priests"?

A. Broom Street Theater.

Q. In the 1989 film *Major League*, Milwaukee County Stadium was the substitute for what baseball stadium?

A. The Cleveland Municipal Stadium.

◆

Q. What 1980 John Belushi-Dan Aykroyd film used shooting locations in southeast Wisconsin?

A. *The Blues Brothers.*

◆

Q. What instrument did Woody Herman play?

A. The clarinet.

◆

Q. What Milwaukee native co-authored *Rose Marie* with Rudolf Friml, wrote the film score for *Naughty Marietta*, and was the long-time musical director of MGM?

A. Herbert Stothart.

◆

Q. What Oshkosh clothing salesman opened a movie theater in 1906 and went on to establish Universal Studios?

A. Carl Laemmle.

◆

Q. What was Milwaukee singer Hildegarde's full name?

A. Hildegarde Sell.

◆

Q. What Broadway musicals did UW-Madison grad Jerry Bock compose?

A. "Fiorello!" (1960) and "She Loves Me" (1963).

Q. Who wrote the book *Big Red*, which was made into a movie of the same name by Disney in 1962?

A. Milwaukee writer Jim Kjelgaard.

Q. On what form of entertainment is Charles ("Chappie") Fox an expert?

A. Circuses (as the long-time director of Circus World Museum in Baraboo and author of several books on circus history).

Q. When did the great Norwegian violinist Ole Bull live in Madison?

A. From 1870 to 1880.

Q. What 1994 Disney release was filmed partially in Interstate State Park?

A. *D2 The Mighty Ducks.*

Q. Where were the railroad scenes in the 1984 film *Mrs. Soffel*, starring Mel Gibson and Diane Keaton, shot?

A. The Mid-Continent Railroad Museum.

Q. What Fort Atkinson coffeehouse is known for folk, jazz, and bluegrass performers?

A. Cafe Carpe.

Q. What Madison duo got a big break when TV's "Northern Exposure" used one of its songs as background music?

A. Two Happy Cowboys from Wisconsin.

Q. What is Wisconsin's largest advertising agency, with income of $21.1 million in 1992?

A. Cramer-Krasselt of Milwaukee.

Q. What is Wisconsin's longest-running folk music radio show?

A. "Simply Folk" (on Wisconsin Public Radio since 1979).

Q. When did "On, Wisconsin" become the official state song?

A. 1959.

Q. What does Elkhorn's Gretsen Company produce?

A. Brass and wind instruments for professional musicians.

Q. Who is the first Wisconsin clown to be inducted into the Clown Hall of Fame?

A. Gene ("Cousin Otto") Lee.

Q. What group dedicated to preserving America's musical and theatrical heritage performs in the Peninsula State Park Amphitheater every summer?

A. The American Folklore Theatre.

Q. In what year did the Ringling Brothers Circus move its headquarters from Baraboo to Sarasota, Florida?

A. 1918.

HISTORY

C H A P T E R   T H R E E

Q. What is the last private residence still standing in which Abraham Lincoln slept?

A. The Tallman House in Janesville.

◆

Q. What did the Menominee Warriors occupy in 1975?

A. The Alexian Brothers Novitiate in Gresham.

◆

Q. What Winnebago chief was forcibly removed from Wisconsin twice and came back each time, beating the troops that transported him west?

A. Chief Yellow Thunder.

◆

Q. Which four "governors" of Wisconsin were not officially governors?

A. Arthur MacArthur (1856), Edward Salomon (1862–64), Walter Goodland (1943–47), and Martin Schreiber (1977–79) all served as acting governor.

◆

Q. Who was Wisconsin's last European-immigrant governor?

A. Julius Heil, governor 1939–43, was born in Germany.

Q. How many justices sit on the Wisconsin Supreme Court?

A. Seven.

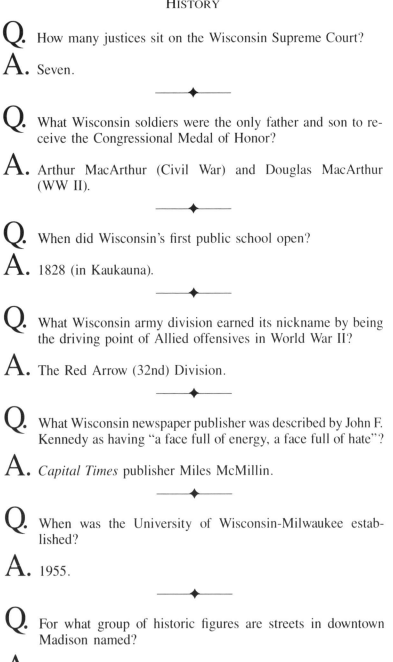

Q. What Wisconsin soldiers were the only father and son to receive the Congressional Medal of Honor?

A. Arthur MacArthur (Civil War) and Douglas MacArthur (WW II).

Q. When did Wisconsin's first public school open?

A. 1828 (in Kaukauna).

Q. What Wisconsin army division earned its nickname by being the driving point of Allied offensives in World War II?

A. The Red Arrow (32nd) Division.

Q. What Wisconsin newspaper publisher was described by John F. Kennedy as having "a face full of energy, a face full of hate"?

A. *Capital Times* publisher Miles McMillin.

Q. When was the University of Wisconsin-Milwaukee established?

A. 1955.

Q. For what group of historic figures are streets in downtown Madison named?

A. Signers of the U.S. Constitution.

Q. What did Wisconsin do without from 1841 to 1853?

A. Banks (the Legislature refused to charter any due to public anti-bank sentiment).

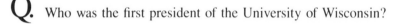

Q. Whom did Joe McCarthy beat in the 1946 U.S. Senate Republican primary?

A. Robert La Follette, Jr.

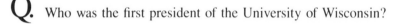

Q. Who was the first president of the University of Wisconsin?

A. John Lathrop (appointed in 1848).

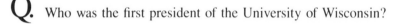

Q. Who held a monopoly on the Wisconsin fur trade in the 1820s and early 1830s?

A. John Jacob Astor's American Fur Company.

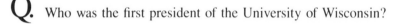

Q. What happened to every one of Wisconsin's more than 100 railroad companies in 1857?

A. They went bankrupt in the national panic of 1857.

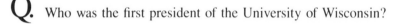

Q. Who was Wisconsin's first public school teacher?

A. Electa Quinney.

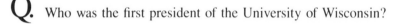

Q. When did the University of Wisconsin and the Wisconsin State University systems merge?

A. 1971.

Q. When did Wisconsin have two governors?

A. 1856 (Republican Coles Bashford and Democrat James Barstow both claimed the election and were sworn in. Bashford was declared the winner.)

Q. How many employees did the State of Wisconsin have on the payroll in 1849?

A. Fourteen.

Q. What does it mean when the U.S. flag is flying over the south or west wings of the Capitol in Madison?

A. That the state Senate (south wing) or Assembly (west wing) is in session.

Q. What does "Court Oreilles," as the French called the Chippewa Indians, mean?

A. "Short ears" (early French explorers thought the Indians somehow mutilated their ears).

Q. What did Byron Kilbourn and Moses Strong do to get a charter for the La Crosse and Milwaukee Railroad in 1856?

A. They bribed fifty-nine state assemblymen, thirteen state senators, and one state supreme court judge.

Q. Who was Ole Kuntson Nattestad?

A. The first Norwegian settler in Wisconsin (1838).

Q. When was Northland College founded in Ashland?

A. 1906 (as a successor to the North Wisconsin Academy).

Q. For how many years were automobiles manufactured in Kenosha?

A. Eighty-six (from 1902 until 1988).

Q. Who was Wisconsin's first pilot?

A. Beloit businessman and aviator Arthur Warner.

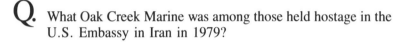

Q. What Wisconsin community was the last to legalize liquor sales?

A. Richland Center (1986).

Q. What Oak Creek Marine was among those held hostage in the U.S. Embassy in Iran in 1979?

A. Kevin Hermening.

Q. What was Wisconsin's first Catholic teaching sisterhood?

A. Sinsiniawa Dominican Sisters (founded in 1847 by Father Samuel Mazzuchelli).

Q. In what year did the Wisconsin Legislature pass the first law giving married women the right to own and control their own property?

A. 1850.

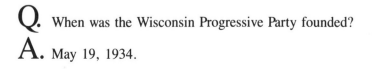

Q. When was the Wisconsin Progressive Party founded?

A. May 19, 1934.

Q. What happened to the original Fort Atkinson?

A. Settlers took it apart and used the logs for houses and river rafts.

———◆———

Q. What Milwaukee woman was chosen by President Clinton to head the U.S. Immigration and Naturalization Service?

A. Doris Meissner.

———◆———

Q. How many auto manufacturing companies occupied the same Kenosha manufacturing facility through the years?

A. Four (Thomas Jeffrey, Nash, American Motors, and Chrysler).

———◆———

Q. What is the oldest law firm in Wisconsin, founded in 1842 as Finch and Lynde?

A. The Milwaukee firm of Foley and Lardner.

———◆———

Q. What important Wisconsin industry did Richard Owens, John Davis, and William Pawlett begin when they opened the first commercial one in Milwaukee in 1840?

A. Brewing.

———◆———

Q. Who were the first Europeans to visit Wisconsin's Lake Superior shore?

A. French fur traders Pierre Radisson and Medart Groseilliers (1658).

———◆———

Q. What profession did Frederick Pabst pursue before he married into a Milwaukee brewing family?

A. He was a steamboat captain on Lake Michigan.

Q. Who was Jacob Best?

A. Founder of the Milwaukee brewery that eventually became Pabst.

———◆———

Q. Of what political party was Milwaukee mayor Daniel Hoan, who served from 1916 until 1940, a member?

A. The Socialist Party.

———◆———

Q. Who planted the first vineyard in Wisconsin?

A. Hungarian Count Agoston Haraszthy.

———◆———

Q. When did Wisconsin open its first out-of-state office to promote the state?

A. 1852 (an office was opened in New York to encourage immigration to Wisconsin).

———◆———

Q. What percentage of Wisconsin's 1890 population of 1.6 million were foreign born?

A. Thirty percent.

———◆———

Q. What type of income tax was Wisconsin the first to levy, in 1911?

A. Corporate income taxes.

———◆———

Q. What type of insurance policy was the first product offered by Employers Mutual of Wausau when it formed in 1911?

A. Workers' compensation.

Q. What was the first college in America founded by Norwegian Lutherans?

A. Luther College (founded in Holmen in 1861 and later moved to Iowa).

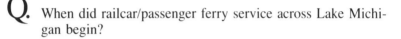

Q. When was the first Wisconsin State Fair held?

A. 1851 (Janesville).

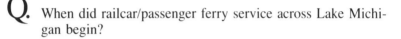

Q. When did railcar/passenger ferry service across Lake Michigan begin?

A. 1892.

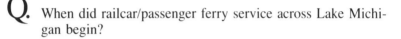

Q. When was the city of La Crosse first settled?

A. 1842 (by Nathan Myrick).

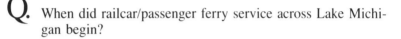

Q. Which University of Wisconsin economist is called the "Father of Social Security"?

A. Edwin Witte.

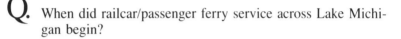

Q. What Wisconsin millionaire and leading Democrat was named by President Grover Cleveland as his Secretary of the Interior?

A. William Freeman Vilas.

Q. What former Wisconsin governor was named by President Benjamin Harrison in 1889 as the first Secretary of Agriculture?

A. Jeremiah Rusk.

Q. What Madison woman co-founded the National Organization for Women?

A. Kathryn Clarenbach.

———◆———

Q. When was the first treaty established between Wisconsin Indian tribes and the U.S. government?

A. 1825 (establishing tribal territories and boundaries).

———◆———

Q. How many times did William Proxmire run for office unsuccessfully before he was elected to the U.S. Senate?

A. Three.

———◆———

Q. What happened in July 1934 during a strike against the Kohler Company?

A. Police shot into a crowd of strikers, killing two and wounding forty-seven.

———◆———

Q. What rumor caused a boom in Kewaunee land prices in 1836?

A. Gold was supposedly discovered.

———◆———

Q. What U.S. senator from Wisconsin became famous for his "Golden Fleece" awards for government waste?

A. William Proxmire.

———◆———

Q. When was the Menominee Reservation established?

A. 1854.

Q. How many women have served Wisconsin in the U.S. House and Senate?

A. None.

Q. What Janesville native became a leader of the Woman's Christian Temperance Union and the suffragist movement?

A. Frances Willard.

Q. How many Wisconsin men served in the Civil War?

A. 91,379 (12,216 died in the war).

Q. How did James Doty persuade the territorial legislature to choose Madison as the permanent Wisconsin capital?

A. He gave free land in Madison to legislators who agreed to vote in favor of Madison.

Q. Why did typesetters at the *Milwaukee Sentinel* go on strike in 1863?

A. To protest the hiring of female typesetters.

Q. When was Fort Howard, at Green Bay, built?

A. 1827.

Q. What was Paul Chadbourne's condition for taking the presidency of the University of Wisconsin in 1867?

A. That women and men attend separate classes and lectures.

Q. Who became the first female professor at Ripon College in 1859?

A. Botany expert Clarissa Tucker Tracy.

Q. What happened to the *Griffin*, the first sailing ship on the Great Lakes?

A. It disappeared without a trace after leaving Washington Island for Montreal in 1679.

Q. What future leader of Israel immigrated to Milwaukee in 1906 and lived there until 1921?

A. Golda Meir.

Q. How did Joseph Schlitz, a bookkeeper, manage to take over a brewery?

A. He married Anna Krug, his boss's widow.

Q. Who attended Milwaukee's West Division High School and in 1898 was appointed to West Point by a Milwaukee congressman?

A. Gen. Douglas MacArthur.

Q. How many members of Wisconsin's thirteen-man Congressional delegation voted against U.S. entry into World War I?

A. Ten of the thirteen (nine in the House, plus Senator Bob La Follette).

Q. What national anti-Catholic, anti-immigrant organization counted 40,000 members in Wisconsin in the mid-1920s?

A. The Ku Klux Klan.

Q. What happened during an 1886 labor union march on the Milwaukee Iron Company?

A. The militia fired into the crowd, killing seven.

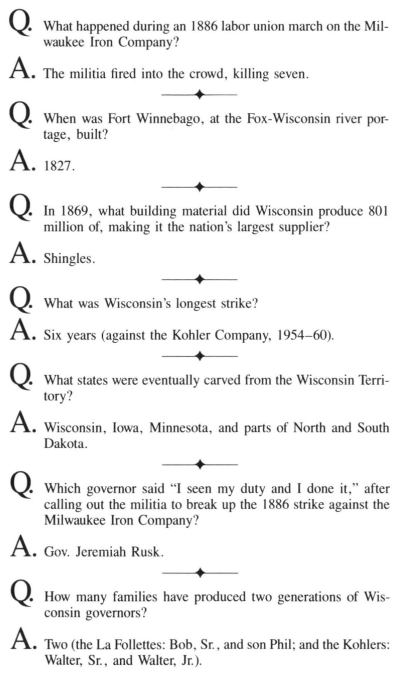

Q. When was Fort Winnebago, at the Fox-Wisconsin river portage, built?

A. 1827.

Q. In 1869, what building material did Wisconsin produce 801 million of, making it the nation's largest supplier?

A. Shingles.

Q. What was Wisconsin's longest strike?

A. Six years (against the Kohler Company, 1954–60).

Q. What states were eventually carved from the Wisconsin Territory?

A. Wisconsin, Iowa, Minnesota, and parts of North and South Dakota.

Q. Which governor said "I seen my duty and I done it," after calling out the militia to break up the 1886 strike against the Milwaukee Iron Company?

A. Gov. Jeremiah Rusk.

Q. How many families have produced two generations of Wisconsin governors?

A. Two (the La Follettes: Bob, Sr., and son Phil; and the Kohlers: Walter, Sr., and Walter, Jr.).

Q. What did the short-lived Bennett Law of 1890 require?

A. That Wisconsin school children be taught only in English.

Q. What was Wisconsin's first insurance company?

A. Northwestern Mutual Life (formed in 1857 in Janesville).

Q. Who was the first Socialist ever elected to the U.S. House of Representatives?

A. Milwaukee congressman Victor Berger (elected to the first of four terms in 1910).

Q. What helped turn public opinion against Senator McCarthy during the 1954 Army-McCarthy hearings?

A. They were broadcast on television.

Q. Who was the first governor of the state of Wisconsin?

A. Nelson Dewey.

Q. What was unusual about Pabst's Pablo brand, Schlitz's Famo label, and Miller's Vivo brand?

A. They were brands of non-alcoholic beer produced by Wisconsin breweries during Prohibition.

Q. Where was the first sawmill on the Wisconsin River built in 1831?

A. At Whitney's Rapids (now Nekoosa).

Q. What 1854 Wisconsin event increased north-south tensions over slavery?

A. A mob freed fugitive slave Joshua Glover from a Milwaukee jail and aided his escape to Canada.

Q. In 1917, what advanced voting method was the Wisconsin State Assembly the first to use?

A. The world's first electric voting machine.

Q. When did Wisconsin pass the nation's first unemployment compensation law?

A. 1932.

Q. When did land acquisition for the Nicolet National Forest begin?

A. 1928.

Q. Which Wisconsin U.S. senator started Earth Day?

A. Gaylord Nelson.

Q. Who was the first woman to receive a law degree from the University of Wisconsin?

A. Belle Case La Follette.

Q. When did the Menominee agree to the Treaty of the Cedars, the first treaty in which Wisconsin's Native American tribes ceded land to the white settlers?

A. 1836.

Q. Who was the first Native American woman to run for state-wide office in Wisconsin?

A. Menominee Ada Deer.

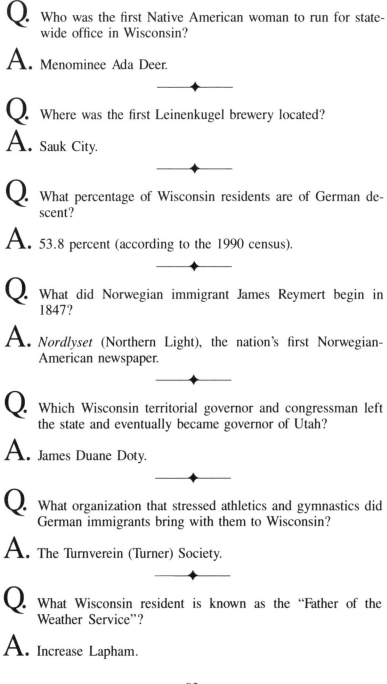

Q. Where was the first Leinenkugel brewery located?

A. Sauk City.

Q. What percentage of Wisconsin residents are of German descent?

A. 53.8 percent (according to the 1990 census).

Q. What did Norwegian immigrant James Reymert begin in 1847?

A. *Nordlyset* (Northern Light), the nation's first Norwegian-American newspaper.

Q. Which Wisconsin territorial governor and congressman left the state and eventually became governor of Utah?

A. James Duane Doty.

Q. What organization that stressed athletics and gymnastics did German immigrants bring with them to Wisconsin?

A. The Turnverein (Turner) Society.

Q. What Wisconsin resident is known as the "Father of the Weather Service"?

A. Increase Lapham.

Q. Who was the first woman to argue a case before the Wisconsin Supreme Court?

A. Milwaukee lawyer Kate Pier (1891).

Q. Which conservation warden did Chicago gangsters try to kill because he arrested them for illegal fishing?

A. Ernie Swift.

Q. What activities are represented on the Wisconsin state seal?

A. Agriculture, mining, navigation, and manufacturing.

Q. What did astronaut Daniel Brandenstein take with him on the space shuttle in 1985?

A. A doorknob from the Wisconsin State Capitol.

Q. How many members are in the Wisconsin State Senate?

A. Thirty-three.

Q. Who led the "Joe Must Go" movement to recall Sen. Joe McCarthy?

A. Sauk City newspaper editor Leroy Gore.

Q. Who served as both first and last (fourth) governor of the Wisconsin Territory?

A. Henry Dodge.

Q. How many members are in the Wisconsin State Assembly?

A. Ninety-nine.

Q. What school was the first in the nation to offer correspondence courses?

A. The University of Wisconsin.

Q. What was Wisconsin's first newspaper?

A. The *Green Bay Intelligencer* (established in 1833).

Q. Who were the first father and son to serve together in the U.S. Senate?

A. Wisconsin Senator Henry Dodge and his son Iowa Senator Augustus Caesar Dodge (from 1848 until 1855).

Q. What is the oldest original pioneer building in Wisconsin?

A. The Tank Cottage in Green Bay, first built in 1776 and remodeled several times during the nineteenth century.

Q. In 1909, who invented the first practical outboard motor?

A. Cambridge native Ole Evinrude.

Q. What is the Wisconsin state motto?

A. Forward.

Q. What was the final battle of the Black Hawk War?

A. The Battle of Bad Axe (on the Mississippi River, August 2, 1832).

Q. When was the first submarine built in the Manitowoc shipyard?

A. 1942.

Q. When Count Haraszthy's Sauk City vineyard failed in 1848, where did he go to begin a new vineyard and start a winemaking industry?

A. California's Napa Valley.

Q. Who gave an unremembered speech about agriculture, education, and hard work at the 1859 Wisconsin State Fair?

A. Abraham Lincoln.

Q. When did the first class enter the University of Wisconsin?

A. February 5, 1849.

Q. When was Wisconsin's ban on colored oleo repealed?

A. 1967.

Q. What custom made the residents of the Indian village of Aztalan, near present-day Lake Mills, unsatisfactory neighbors?

A. Cannibalism.

Q. When did the Legislature approve Wisconsin's first highway beautification programs?

A. 1931.

Q. Where did future Confederate President Jefferson Davis first meet Robert Anderson, future commander of Fort Sumter, in 1830?

A. Fort Crawford at Prairie du Chien.

Q. When did Robert La Follette first become governor?

A. 1901.

Q. In what battle did Chief Black Hawk and fifty Sauk and Fox warriors hold off and escape from a force of 1,000 army troops?

A. The Battle of Wisconsin Heights (near Sauk City, July 21, 1832).

Q. Who was the first woman elected to statewide office?

A. Mrs. Dena Smith (elected Treasurer in 1960).

Q. After Joseph Schlitz died in a shipwreck, who took over the Schlitz brewery?

A. The six Uihlein boys (Mrs. Schlitz's nephews).

Q. When were women first admitted to the University of Wisconsin?

A. 1866.

Q. When did protesters led by Father Groppi take over the State Assembly Chamber in the Capitol?

A. 1969.

Q. Who was the first European to set foot in what is now Wisconsin in 1634?

A. Jean Nicolet.

Q. Where did Jean Nicolet land?

A. Near Red Banks, on the eastern shore of Green Bay.

Q. Who were the first Europeans to build a dwelling in Wisconsin in 1658?

A. Pierre Esprit Radisson and Medart Chouart des Groseillers (on the west shore of Chequamegon Bay).

Q. When did Wisconsin become a state?

A. May 29, 1848.

Q. What is the oldest community in Wisconsin?

A. Green Bay (settled in 1764).

Q. What early settler, trader, and military leader is called the "Father of Wisconsin"?

A. Charles de Langlade.

Q. What did Father Claude Allouez build on the shore of Che-quamegon Bay in 1665?

A. The first Christian place of worship in Wisconsin.

———◆———

Q. When was the State Historical Society of Wisconsin founded?

A. 1846.

———◆———

Q. What is the second oldest community in Wisconsin?

A. Prairie du Chien (settled in 1781).

———◆———

Q. When did Marquette and Jolliet make their famous journey down the Fox, Wisconsin, and Mississippi rivers?

A. 1673.

———◆———

Q. What future U.S. president served as a private in the army that chased Black Hawk and his band of Sauk Indians through southern Wisconsin in 1832?

A. Abraham Lincoln.

———◆———

Q. What was Wisconsin's largest military training and staging area during the Civil War?

A. Camp Randall in Madison.

———◆———

Q. What former Speaker of the Wisconsin Assembly was named Ambassador to Norway by President Clinton in 1993?

A. Tom Loftus.

Q. What is John McCaffary's claim to fame?

A. He is the only person ever executed in Wisconsin (1851).

Q. Who founded the Progressive faction of the Republican Party?

A. Robert La Follette, Sr.

Q. What is the oldest photography studio in the United States in continuous existence?

A. The H. H. Bennett Photo Studio of Wisconsin Dells.

Q. What is the most devastating forest fire in American history?

A. The Peshtigo fire, October 8, 1871, which destroyed forests, villages, and farms throughout northeast Wisconsin.

Q. What happened to the Lake Michigan schooner *Rouse Simmons*, known as the Christmas tree ship?

A. It sank off Kewanee in a storm on November 23, 1912.

Q. During the Civil War, what animal was the mascot of Company C of the 8th Wisconsin Volunteers?

A. Old Abe, the war eagle.

Q. What new approach to warfare did Milwaukee's Billy Mitchell espouse?

A. Development of air power.

Q. What was the last American battleship ever launched?

A. The *Wisconsin* (launched in 1942).

———◆———

Q. What technological innovations allowed Milwaukee's nineteenth-century breweries to dominate the American market?

A. Pasteurization and large-scale bottling techniques that prevented spoilage.

———◆———

Q. How many acres burned in the Peshtigo fire?

A. 1,280,000 acres in six counties.

———◆———

Q. In 1869, who built the first practical typewriter?

A. Kenosha reporter Christopher Latham Sholes, working in a Milwaukee machine shop.

———◆———

Q. What pioneering social legislation was Wisconsin the first state to pass in 1911?

A. Workers' compensation insurance.

———◆———

Q. When were women first allowed to argue cases before the Wisconsin Supreme Court?

A. In 1877.

———◆———

Q. In what year did Wisconsin lead the world in lumber production?

A. 1899 (four billion board feet).

Q. Where was the first capital of the Wisconsin Territory?

A. Belmont.

Q. For what 1842 act is Wisconsin territorial legislator James Vineyard known?

A. Shooting and killing fellow legislator C. C. Arndt during a debate.

Q. What future president was in command of Fort Crawford in the mid-1830s?

A. Zachary Taylor.

Q. What did the Menominee give up under the Treaty of the Cedars?

A. 4,000,000 acres of land.

Q. Where did the Republican Party begin?

A. At the Ripon Schoolhouse (1854).

Q. What did Wisconsin begin doing to its highways in 1917 that no other state had ever done?

A. Creating a uniform highway numbering system.

Q. Who is the only Wisconsin governor to die in a war?

A. Governor Louis Harvey drowned leading an 1862 relief contingent to Union forces in Tennessee.

Q. What is Wisconsin's oldest college?

A. Carroll College (opened in 1846).

Q. What organization began in Boscobel in 1899?

A. The Gideons.

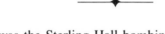

Q. In 1886, Wisconsin's women voters were given the right to vote in what kind of elections?

A. Those pertaining to school matters.

Q. When was the Sterling Hall bombing?

A. 1970.

Q. What was "The Beer That Made Milwaukee Famous"?

A. Schlitz (which coined the slogan in 1872).

Q. Who was the first woman to apply to practice before the Wisconsin Supreme Court?

A. Janesville lawyer Rhoda Lavinia Gooddell (she applied in 1875 but was refused).

———◆———

Q. How many people died in the Peshtigo fire?

A. Between 1,200 and 1,300.

Q. How many breweries operated by the Walters family were in Wisconsin?

A. Four (Geo. Walter Brewing of Appleton, Walter Bros. Brewing of Menasha, Walters Brewing of Eau Claire, and West Bend Lithia Company).

Q. When did Wisconsin abolish capital punishment?

A. 1853.

Q. When was the Wisconsin Woman's Suffrage Association organized?

A. 1882.

Q. For what is the Atheneum Corporation, founded in Milwaukee in 1886, remembered?

A. It was the world's first stock company created solely by and for women.

Q. When was Ripon College founded?

A. 1851.

Q. For what is Poplar native Richard Bong remembered?

A. Shooting down forty enemy aircraft during World War II, making him America's leading air ace.

Q. Who was Wisconsin's first millionaire?

A. Hercules Dousman made his fortune as a fur trader in the 1830s.

Q. Where was the nation's first Christian Science Church?

A. Oconto (the building was dedicated in 1887).

———◆———

Q. What was the major funding source for Milwaukee's immigrant settlement house in the early 1900s?

A. Sales of *The Settlement Cookbook* (first published in 1901 and still in print).

———◆———

Q. Who was the head of the Wisconsin Free Library Commission from 1895 to 1914?

A. Lutie Stearns, who established more than 150 public libraries.

———◆———

Q. To what crime did Lawrencia Bembenek, famous for her escape from Taycheedah Correctional Institution, plead guilty?

A. None (she pleaded "no contest" to second-degree murder).

———◆———

Q. In a 1912 referendum, the men of Wisconsin voted 227,054 to 135,736 against what?

A. Allowing women to vote.

———◆———

Q. The Women's International League for Peace and Freedom successfully lobbied the 1923 Wisconsin Legislature to do what?

A. Abolish compulsory military training at the University of Wisconsin.

———◆———

Q. When Jean Nicolet landed in Wisconsin, what did he do to impress the Winnebagos who greeted him?

A. Fired two pistols in the air.

Q. Who took over the family brewery on her husband's death in 1878, making her one of the first female corporate presidents in America?

A. Johanna Heileman.

———◆———

Q. Who led the fight to allow the Chippewa to stay on their northern Wisconsin lands when the U.S. government wanted to move them west in the early 1850s?

A. The Rev. L. H. Wheeler.

———◆———

Q. What was Wisconsin's first coeducational college?

A. Lawrence Academy (later a university), founded in 1854.

———◆———

Q. According to a 1913 legislative study, what was the most lucrative profession for a woman in Superior?

A. Prostitution (prostitutes made $15–$40 weekly, two to four times more than women in factories and retail stores).

———◆———

Q. What were the men who bombed Sterling Hall on the UW-Madison campus protesting?

A. The Vietnam War.

———◆———

Q. What Wisconsin governor resigned in 1977 to become U.S. Ambassador to Mexico?

A. Patrick Lucey.

———◆———

Q. When was Beloit College founded?

A. 1846.

Q. Who was the first woman to serve on the Wisconsin Supreme Court?

A. Shirley Abrahamson.

———◆———

Q. When did Wisconsin's first cheese factory open?

A. 1864.

———◆———

Q. Who was John Anderson's running mate in his 1980 third-party presidential bid?

A. Former Wisconsin Governor Patrick Lucey.

———◆———

Q. What Wisconsin congressman was President Clinton's first Secretary of Defense?

A. Les Aspin.

———◆———

Q. Where was the American flag first raised over Wisconsin territory following the War of 1812?

A. At Fort Crawford in Prairie du Chien (1814).

———◆———

Q. What Chancellor of UW-Madison was named Secretary of Health and Human Services by President Clinton?

A. Donna Shalala.

———◆———

Q. Where was Governor Lucius Fairchild when word of the Peshtigo fire reached Madison on October 9, 1871?

A. In Chicago assisting victims of the great Chicago fire.

Q. When was the treaty signed with the Chippewa Indians creating three reservations for the tribe at Odanah, Lac Court Oreilles, and Lac du Flambeau?

A. 1854.

———◆———

Q. What former Wisconsin congressman was named Secretary of Defense by President Nixon?

A. Melvin Laird.

———◆———

Q. Who represents Wisconsin in Statuary Hall in the U.S. Capitol?

A. Robert La Follette, Sr., and Father Jacques Marquette.

———◆———

Q. What was the route of the world's first auto race, held in 1878?

A. Green Bay to Madison.

———◆———

Q. When was Wisconsin's first 4-H Club organized?

A. 1914 (near Lake Geneva).

———◆———

Q. When did German immigrant Frederick Miller begin his Milwaukee brewery?

A. 1855 (he bought the Plank Road Brewery from the Best family).

———◆———

Q. Who was the first presidential candidate from Wisconsin?

A. Robert La Follette (as a Progressive, in 1924).

Q. Who is known as the "Father of the Automobile"?

A. Rev. John Carhart of Racine (built a steam-powered buggy in 1871).

———◆———

Q. When did Margarethe Schurz begin the first kindergarten in America?

A. 1856 (in Watertown).

———◆———

Q. What Milwaukee janitor shot Alabama Governor George Wallace during the 1972 presidential campaign?

A. Arthur Bremer.

———◆———

Q. When Jack Vilas took off from an airstrip near Boulder Junction in 1915, how was he making history?

A. By making the nation's first fire patrol flight.

———◆———

Q. Madison native Richard Lamm became governor of what state?

A. Colorado.

———◆———

Q. What Marinette man's 1986 plane crash in Nicaragua led to exposure of the Iran-Contra affair?

A. Eugene Hasenfus.

———◆———

Q. What state did Madison native Wayne Morse represent in the U.S. Senate?

A. Oregon.

Q. Where was Wisconsin's first post office?

A. Green Bay (1821).

Q. Who was the first Republican governor of Wisconsin?

A. Coles Bashford (from 1856 to 1858).

Q. Which company bought the first workers' compensation insurance, following passage of Wisconsin's pioneering legislation?

A. Wausau Sulphate Fibre Company (since renamed Mosinee Paper Corp.).

Q. What activity caused the first rush of immigrants to Wisconsin?

A. Lead mining, which caused a jump in population in the southwest part of the state from the 1820s to the 1840s.

Q. Who began the first permanent European settlement on Madeline Island?

A. Michel Cadotte (1793).

Q. What Ripon native became a leader in the women's suffrage movement, working with Susan B. Anthony?

A. Carrie Chapman Catt.

Q. When was the last log drive down the Mississippi River?

A. 1915.

Q. What was Robert La Follette, Sr.'s nickname?

A. "Fighting Bob."

Q. What was Jean Nicolet looking for when he stepped ashore in 1634?

A. The Northwest Passage to the Orient.

Q. When was the first paper mill built on the Wisconsin River?

A. 1887 (at Wisconsin Rapids).

Q. What tribe did the Chippewa drive from Wisconsin at the Battle of Mole Lake?

A. The Sioux.

Q. Where was Wisconsin's first Lutheran Church founded in 1840?

A. Near Theinsville.

Q. How many Wisconsin citizens have received the Congressional Medal of Honor?

A. Sixty-two.

Q. What journalistic technique did H. H. Bennett pioneer?

A. Photojournalism.

Q. Which 1980 presidential candidate held an outdoor extravaganza directed by Francis Ford Coppola on the Capitol square in Madison?

A. Democrat Jerry Brown.

———◆———

Q. Who was the first woman elected to the Wisconsin State Senate?

A. Democrat Kathryn Morrison of Platteville (1974).

———◆———

Q. When did the Oneida tribe come to Wisconsin?

A. Beginning in 1821 (they received their reservation near Green Bay in 1838).

———◆———

Q. For what purpose was St. Norbert College founded in 1898?

A. To train priests.

———◆———

Q. Who claimed to be the "Lost Dauphin," son of the French king Louis XVI?

A. Eleazer Williams (settled near De Pere in 1821).

———◆———

Q. Members of what Indian tribe accompanied Jean Nicolet on his first trip to Wisconsin?

A. Hurons.

———◆———

Q. Who was the first woman to be re-elected to the Wisconsin State Senate?

A. Republican Susan Engeleiter.

Q. Which governor-elect died before taking office?

A. Orland Loomis (elected in November 1942, died in December 1942).

———◆———

Q. What powered the autos in the world's first auto race?

A. Steam.

———◆———

Q. Who was the first woman in America appointed circuit court commissioner?

A. Milwaukee lawyer Kate Hamilton Pier, mother of Kate Pier (1891).

———◆———

Q. What was Fort St. Francis?

A. A fort built near the mouth of the Fox River by the French in the 1670s.

———◆———

Q. Where was Joe McCarthy born?

A. Grand Chute.

———◆———

Q. Who first coined the phrase "On, Wisconsin"?

A. Nineteen-year-old Arthur MacArthur, as he led the 24th Wisconsin Infantry in a charge up Missionary Ridge, Nov. 24, 1863.

———◆———

Q. Before Governor Tommy Thompson became the state's longest-serving governor in January 1994, who held that record?

A. Governor Jeremiah Rusk (January 2, 1882 to January 7, 1889).

Q. In what years did the Progressive Party control the state legislature?

A. In the 1935 and 1937 sessions.

———◆———

Q. Who was Wisconsin's first Democratic governor?

A. Nelson Dewey (elected in 1848).

———◆———

Q. How many political parties have Wisconsin's governors represented?

A. Four (Whig, Democratic, Republican, and Progressive).

———◆———

Q. What was Sen. Joe McCarthy's self-imposed, and undeserved, nickname?

A. Tail-Gunner Joe.

———◆———

Q. What was the advertising slogan for Pabst Beer in the 1890s?

A. "He drinks Best who drinks Pabst."

———◆———

Q. Who was the first governor of Wisconsin who was born and raised in the state?

A. Robert La Follette.

———◆———

Q. What presidential candidate was the object of an assassination attempt during a visit to Milwaukee in 1912?

A. Bull Moose candidate Theodore Roosevelt.

ARTS & LITERATURE

CHAPTER FOUR

Q. Who wrote the hymn "In the Sweet Bye and Bye"?

A. Elkhorn composer Joseph Philbrick Webster (music) and Sanford Fillmore Bennett (lyrics).

Q. What self-taught Madison artist is known for "assemblages" of marbles, shells, beads, and found objects?

A. Simon Sparrow.

Q. On what Wisconsin governor did August Derleth base his novel *Shadow on the Glass*?

A. Nelson Dewey.

Q. In what small Wisconsin town was Frank Lloyd Wright born?

A. Richland Center (in 1867).

Q. What did Wausau's Philosopher Press, founded in 1896 by Helen and Phillip VanVechten and William Ellis, produce?

A. Handprinted, limited edition books.

Q. Who designed the Milwaukee County War Memorial building?

A. Eero Saarinen.

Q. What is architecturally unusual about the Richards House in Watertown?

A. It is the largest octagon-shaped house in Wisconsin.

Q. What is the oldest building on Marquette University's campus?

A. The Joan of Arc Chapel, a fifteenth-century French church moved to the campus in 1965.

Q. For what is Gustav Stickley, born in Osceola in 1858, best known?

A. His work in the arts and crafts movement and his furniture designs.

Q. Why did Madison poet William Ellery Leonard seldom leave home?

A. He was afflicted with agoraphobia (the fear of open spaces).

Q. Millville Township produced what well-known science fiction writer?

A. Clifford D. Simak.

Q. What New Glarus writer won the 1956 National Book Award for nonfiction for *American in Italy*?

A. Herbert Kubly.

Q. What was the name of the Waukesha County estate of actors Alfred Lunt and Lynn Fontanne?

A. Ten Chimneys.

———◆———

Q. Where did author Edna Ferber grow up?

A. Appleton.

———◆———

Q. Who designed the S. C. Johnson Company Administration Building and the S. C. Johnson Research Tower in Racine?

A. Frank Lloyd Wright.

———◆———

Q. What unusual building material was used for the Iron Block at the corner of East Wisconsin Avenue and Water Street in Milwaukee?

A. The facade is prefabricated cast iron (ordered from an eastern company and sent to Milwaukee by boat).

———◆———

Q. What school offered the nation's first college course using silk screening as an art medium?

A. UW-Madison (in 1951).

———◆———

Q. What artist contributed both paintings and money to create an art center for Door County?

A. Gerhard C. F. Miller (for the Miller Art Center).

———◆———

Q. What famous landscape architect designed Milwaukee's Lake Park?

A. Frederick Law Olmstead.

Q. Which University of Wisconsin professor of engineering gave Frank Lloyd Wright his first job?

A. Allan Conover.

———◆———

Q. Where did much of the building materials for Milwaukee's St. Josaphat Basilica come from?

A. The main post office and an old courthouse, both in Chicago.

———◆———

Q. Who designed the Farmers and Merchants Bank in Columbus in 1919?

A. Louis Sullivan.

———◆———

Q. What Waunakee poet and novelist was famous for the lines "Laugh, and the world laughs with you; weep, and you weep alone"?

A. Ella Wheeler Wilcox (1850–1919).

———◆———

Q. Where did Stephen Ambrose, historian and expert on presidents Eisenhower and Nixon, grow up?

A. Whitewater.

———◆———

Q. Who created the statue "Wisconsin" atop the Wisconsin Capitol?

A. Daniel Chester French, creator of the Lincoln statue in the Lincoln Memorial in Washington, DC.

———◆———

Q. How did the UW-Madison School of Business assist the arts in 1968?

A. By offering the nation's first graduate program in arts administration.

Q. Where was writer Hamlin Garland born?

A. West Salem (1860).

———◆———

Q. Ten Chimneys is the home of what artistic group?

A. The American Inside Theater.

———◆———

Q. What newspaperman and humorist grew up in Grantsburg and made his mark with the 1882 book *Forty Liars and Other Lies*?

A. Edgar Wilson ("Bill") Nye (1850–1896).

———◆———

Q. What is the nation's only Frank Lloyd Wright-designed house open for overnight rentals?

A. The Seth Peterson Cottage (in Mirror Lake State Park near Wisconsin Dells).

———◆———

Q. Where is the world's largest collection of manuscripts and papers of Hobbit creator J. R. R. Tolkien?

A. Marquette University.

———◆———

Q. What famous author of children's books wrote the 1935 *Little House in the Big Woods* about Wisconsin?

A. Laura Ingalls Wilder.

———◆———

Q. What book did Juliette Kinzie write about her experiences in 1830s Portage?

A. *Wau-bun: The Early Days in the Northwest* (1856).

Q. What Zona Gale protégée and acclaimed short-story writer led a communal living experiment near Portage in 1931?

A. Margery Latimer.

Q. Where did writer Ben Hecht grow up?

A. Racine.

Q. What Rhinelander writer's 1969 book *Arrow in the Sun* was adapted for the 1970 film *Soldier Blue*?

A. Theodore Victor Olson.

Q. Who invented the wall-hung toilet?

A. Frank Lloyd Wright.

Q. What Edna Ferber novel takes place in the northwoods logging camps and the Fox River paper mills?

A. *Come and Get It.*

Q. What central Wisconsin town is the setting for Glenway Wescott's 1927 novel *The Grandmothers*?

A. Ripon.

Q. Who is the state's most prolific writer, author of more than 150 books as well as articles, short stories, and poetry?

A. August Derleth.

Q. What is the name of Frank Lloyd Wright's Spring Green home?

A. Taliesin (which means "shining brow" in Welsh).

Q. What St. Croix Falls native received the 1940 Pulitzer Prize for his eight-volume biography of Woodrow Wilson?

A. Ray Stannard Baker.

Q. Where did artist Georgia O'Keefe grow up?

A. Sun Prairie and Madison.

Q. Where is George Vukelich's 1962 novel *Fisherman's Beach* set?

A. Manitowoc and Two Rivers.

Q. Arcadia and the surrounding countryside were the setting for what 1977 occult novel by Peter Straub?

A. *If You Could See Me Now*.

Q. What did Carl Sandburg do when he lived in Wisconsin from 1902 to 1912?

A. He served as organizer for the Social-Democratic Party and secretary to Milwaukee Mayor Seidel.

Q. Where was Thorstein Veblen (1857–1929), author and lecturer famous for his 1899 book *The Theory of the Leisure Class*, born?

A. Valders.

Q. Why is the A. D. German Warehouse in Richland Center unique among Frank Lloyd Wright's works?

A. It is the only warehouse he ever designed.

Q. In what small Wisconsin River town did writer August Derleth live his entire life?

A. Sauk City (1909–1971).

Q. Where is the state's largest concentration of prairie style architecture?

A. La Crosse, with more than 100 such buildings.

Q. Edna Ferber won a 1925 Pulitzer Prize for what novel?

A. *So Big.*

Q. Where was author Laura Ingalls Wilder born?

A. Pepin.

Q. Who designed the Milwaukee City Hall and the Pfister Hotel?

A. Henry C. Koch.

Q. Where does the 1935 children's classic *Caddie Woodlawn* take place?

A. On a pioneer homestead in Downsville (near Menomonie).

Q. What resources are available to artists in residence at the John Michael Kohler Arts Center in Kohler?

A. Anything used in the Kohler plumbing fixtures factory (including the craftsmen who work there).

Q. Where is the original of the famous sculpture "The End of the Trail" by James Earl Fraser?

A. In a park in downtown Waupun.

Q. What materials did ex-lumberjack Fred Smith use to create the larger-than-life sculptures on display in a park in Phillips?

A. Concrete and broken glass.

Q. What museum has the annual "Birds in Art" exhibit?

A. The Leigh Yawkey Woodson Art Museum in Wausau.

Q. What Racine author wrote an award-winning 1979 account of his mother's life as an Armenian immigrant?

A. David Kherdian.

Q. Who created the shrines, grottos, and sculptures of the Dickeyville Grotto?

A. Father Mathias Wernerus and his cousin Mary Wernerus.

Q. For what is Neenah's Bergstrom-Mahler Museum known?

A. Its collection of more than 1,700 glass paperweights.

Q. What nineteenth-century poet, author of "Silver Threads Among the Gold," spent most of his life in Shiocton?

A. Eben Rexford.

Q. What opera had its world premiere in Madison in 1993?

A. *Shining Brow* (based on the life of Frank Lloyd Wright).

Q. What Wisconsin community is known for its pottery studios, including Rockdale Union Stoneware and Rowe Pottery Works?

A. Cambridge.

Q. On what Wisconsin daily did Edna Ferber and Zona Gale work as reporters?

A. The *Milwaukee Journal*.

Q. What annual award recognizes the most significant book by a Wisconsin author published during the previous year?

A. The Banta.

Q. Where are Alfred Lunt and Lynn Fontanne buried?

A. Forest Home Cemetery in Milwaukee.

Q. Who wrote *We Are Incredible* (1928), *Nellie Bloom and Other Stories* (1929), and *This Is My Body* (1931)?

A. Portage author Margery Latimer.

Q. Madison writer George Vukelich's popular columns describe conversations in what northern Wisconsin establishment?

A. The American Legion Bar in Three Lakes.

Q. What nationally known environmental writer was associated with Northland College in Ashland?

A. Sigurd Olson.

Q. What was Aldo Leopold's most famous work?

A. *A Sand County Almanac*.

Q. Where is the world's largest circus archive?

A. Circus World Museum Library and Resource Center in Baraboo.

Q. What *Milwaukee Journal* outdoor writer's books *Wild Goose, Brother Goose*, and *Flight of the White Wolf* were made into movies?

A. Mel Ellis.

Q. What Dodgeville poet won the 1976 National League of American Pen Women prize for *The Ineluctable Sea*?

A. Edna Meudt.

Q. What Door County author writes his books in a converted chicken coop?

A. Norbert Blei.

Q. What was the name of the raccoon Edgerton author Sterling North made famous in his 1963 bestseller?

A. Rascal.

---◆---

Q. Where was Frank Lloyd Wright originally buried?

A. In the cemetery of Unity Chapel (across from Taliesin).

---◆---

Q. What internationally famous poet lived virtually her entire life on Blackhawk Island in Lake Koshkonong?

A. Lorine Niedecker.

---◆---

Q. Who is the only Wisconsin author ever featured on the cover of *Time*?

A. Fort Atkinson mystery writer Craig Rice (January 28, 1946).

---◆---

Q. What is the setting for Ben Logan's 1975 classic *The Land Remembers*?

A. Gays Mills and the Kickapoo Valley.

---◆---

Q. What was the first book to be printed in Wisconsin?

A. An 1834 Chippewa almanac written by a missionary, Father Samuel Mazzuchelli.

---◆---

Q. What Hazel Green native won both the Pulitzer Prize and the National Book Award for his 1969 biography *Huey Long*?

A. T. Harry Williams.

Q. What eminent nineteenth-century poet, geologist, and linguist is buried in Hazel Green Cemetery?

A. James Gates Percival.

Q. What Footville woman wrote the 1912 children's classic *The Little Engine That Could*?

A. Frances Wiggins Ford.

Q. Who was UW-Madison's first artist in residence?

A. Painter John Steuart Curry (from 1936 to 1946).

Q. Where did novelist Irving Wallace grow up?

A. Kenosha.

Q. What Kewaskum native, one of the "lost generation" of American writers in Paris, wrote *Goodbye, Wisconsin* (1928)?

A. Glenway Wescott.

Q. George Peck, author of the *Peck's Bad Boy* stories of the late 1800s, held what elective offices?

A. Mayor of Milwaukee (1890) and Governor of Wisconsin (1891–95).

Q. In what poetry contest sponsored by UW-Madison are the winner's poems published by the UW Press?

A. The Brittingham Prize.

Q. For what was Frank Lloyd Wright's sister, Maginel Wright Barney, known?

A. She was an artist and illustrator of books and magazines.

Q. What UW-Whitewater professor has produced award-winning biographies of George Bernard Shaw, Mrs. Patrick Campbell, and Charlotte Brontë?

A. Margot Peters.

Q. What UW-Madison professor's 1893 paper, "The Significance of the Frontier in American History," made him a leading historian?

A. Frederick Jackson Turner.

Q. What director of the State Historical Society in the 1890s translated seventy-three volumes of journals of seventeenth- and eighteenth-century French Jesuit missionaries?

A. Reuben Gold Thwaites.

Q. What is the setting for Wallace Stegner's 1987 novel *Crossing to Safety*?

A. Madison.

Q. What world-famous photographer's first photographs were of 1890s Milwaukee?

A. Edward Steichen.

Q. What 1844 book was the first one written by a Wisconsin resident and published in Wisconsin?

A. *A Geographical and Topographical Description of Wisconsin*, by Increase Lapham.

Q. Who wrote the book that Alfred Hitchcock turned into 1960's *Psycho*?

A. Milwaukeean Robert Bloch.

———◆———

Q. Where is much of Peter Straub's 1988 best-selling novel *Koko* set?

A. Milwaukee.

———◆———

Q. What did Margaret H'Doubler organize at UW-Madison in 1926?

A. The nation's first major in dance education.

———◆———

Q. What two hit plays by actor and writer Larry Shue were first performed by the Milwaukee Repertory Theater?

A. *The Nerd* (1981) and *The Foreigner* (1983).

———◆———

Q. What Milwaukee linguist and diplomat is best known for his translation of *Quo Vadis* from Polish to English?

A. Jeremiah Curtin.

———◆———

Q. What monumental work on the American language is UW-Madison professor Frederic Cassidy compiling?

A. *The Dictionary of American Regional English.*

———◆———

Q. Where is the only monument in the United States that honors the German poets, philosophers, and dramatists Goethe and Schiller?

A. Washington Park in Milwaukee (unveiled in 1908).

Q. Who wrote *The House on Jefferson Street* (1971), describing his boyhood in turn-of-the-century Milwaukee?

A. Horace Gregory.

Q. Who were the heroes of Milwaukee author Frederic Brown's private eye series published from 1947 to 1963?

A. Ed and Am Hunter.

Q. Who are the subjects of Madison author Margaret George's pair of best-selling historical novels?

A. King Henry VIII and Mary, Queen of Scots.

Q. What Madison sculptor got an 1866 commission for a statue of Abraham Lincoln for the U.S. Capitol rotunda?

A. Vinnie Ream Hoxie (the first woman to receive such a commission).

Q. What Thornton Wilder play was made into the musical *Hello, Dolly*?

A. *The Matchmaker*.

Q. What twenty-year-old Oshkosh sculptor created the "Genius of Wisconsin," the center of the Wisconsin Building at the 1893 Columbian Exposition, now on display in the State Capitol?

A. Helen Farnsworth Mears.

Q. What Milwaukee-born architect first recognized the genius of Frank Lloyd Wright and published the first article about Wright's work in 1900?

A. Robert Spencer.

Q. What Milwaukee sculptor's metal wire sculptures are in New York's Lincoln Center and the Air and Space Museum in Washington, DC?

A. Richard Lippold.

Q. Where did prizewinning author Saul Bellow attend college?

A. UW-Madison.

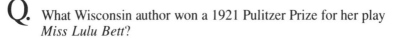

Q. What Wisconsin author won a 1921 Pulitzer Prize for her play *Miss Lulu Bett*?

A. Zona Gale.

Q. What does the statue "Wisconsin" on top of the Capitol dome have on her head?

A. A helmet adorned with a badger between two cornucopias, with an ear of corn over each of her ears.

Q. Who designed the current Wisconsin State Capitol?

A. New York architect George Post.

Q. What then-risqué 1883 book made writer Ella Wheeler Wilcox rich and famous?

A. *Poems of Passion.*

Q. What happened to the State Capitol on February 27, 1904?

A. It burned (resulting in a total loss of the building).

Q. What Milwaukee native is famous for her books about horses, especially the 1947 novel *Misty of Chincoteaque*?

A. Marguerite Henry.

———◆———

Q. In addition to *The Land Remembers*, Ben Logan is the author of what 1983 novel set in the same locale?

A. *The Empty Meadow.*

———◆———

Q. What engineering feat is depicted in the mural in the Wisconsin State Senate chambers?

A. Completion of the Panama Canal.

———◆———

Q. How many inches shorter than the national Capitol is the Wisconsin Capitol dome?

A. Seventeen.

———◆———

Q. What is the focus of the collection at the Bradley Sculpture Garden?

A. Modern sculpture.

———◆———

Q. For what work did Hamlin Garland win the 1922 Pulitzer Prize for fiction?

A. *A Daughter of the Middle Border.*

———◆———

Q. Where is the only statue of Abraham Lincoln sitting with his wife standing next to him?

A. Racine.

Q. What event brings classical musicians from all over the nation to Fish Creek every summer?

A. The Peninsula Music Festival.

———◆———

Q. What well-known landscape architect built The Clearing near Ellison Bay as an artists' retreat?

A. Jens Jensen.

———◆———

Q. Who was the real-life model for Caddie Woodlawn?

A. Caroline Woodhouse, grandmother of the author.

———◆———

Q. What Milwaukee architect worked for Frank Lloyd Wright from 1914 to 1917 before beginning his own career in southeast Wisconsin?

A. Russell Barr Williamson.

———◆———

Q. What UW-Madison artist in residence from 1948 to 1974 was known for collage-like paintings called "magic realism"?

A. Aaron Bohrod.

———◆———

Q. What Washington Island summer school teaches weaving, spinning, dyeing, quilting, and knitting?

A. Sievers School of Fiber Arts.

———◆———

Q. Where did the Pro Arte Quartet play before it took up residence at UW-Madison?

A. Belgium (the Belgian Royal Court Quartet fled in 1940 to escape the German army).

Q. What is the most expensive work in the UW-Madison's Elvehjem Museum of Art?

A. A painting by Italian Bernardo Strozzi (cost: $1 million).

Q. Where did Marjorie Kinnan Rawlings, author of *The Yearling* and other novels about Florida, attend college?

A. UW-Madison.

Q. What nationally known wildlife artist spent a forty-year first career working for the Milwaukee Public Museum?

A. Owen Gromme.

Q. Who has been managing director of the Milwaukee Repertory Theater since 1974?

A. Sara O'Connor.

Q. Who wrote the melody for the Civil War tune "Lorena"?

A. Elkhorn composer Joseph Philbrick Webster.

Q. How much did the state Capitol building originally cost?

A. $7,259,000.

Q. Who wrote the popular "Little Brown Church in the Vale," an 1857 hymn about a church in Iowa?

A. William Pitts of Rock County.

Q. Who wrote the turn-of-the-century hit "After the Ball"?

A. Milwaukee songwriter Charles Harris.

Q. Why were Frank Lloyd Wright's remains exhumed and moved?

A. His widow's will requested that Wright be buried with her in Arizona.

Q. On what instrument did Neenah native Arthur Shattuck (1881–1951) achieve international fame?

A. The piano (playing with the New York Philharmonic and throughout Europe).

Q. Where did Zona Gale live and find inspiration for many of her characters and stories?

A. Portage.

Q. What Milwaukee-born novelist's works, including *Any Number Can Play* and *My Life on Earth*, were all set in Wisconsin?

A. Edward Harris Heth.

Q. Where is the setting for Mark Schorer's novel *A House Too Old*?

A. Sauk City (Schorer's hometown).

Q. Who created the Solar Pons mystery series?

A. August Derleth.

Q. Who founded the Rhinelander School of the Arts in 1964?

A. Writer Robert Gard.

◆

Q. What was the first novel published by a Wisconsin author?

A. *Bachelor Ben* (by Madison author Augusta Giles, in 1875).

◆

Q. What Milwaukee native wrote a series of Pulitzer Prize-winning books on Russia in the 1950s after serving as U.S. Ambassador to the Soviet Union?

A. George Kennan.

◆

Q. Whom did Lillian Steichen, Edward Steichen's sister, marry in 1908?

A. Carl Sandburg.

◆

Q. Who wrote the archaeology books *The Mute Stones Speak* (1960) and *The Greek Stones Speak* (1962)?

A. UW-Madison classics professor Paul Mac Kendrick.

◆

Q. What Milwaukee lawyer authored several books on public policy and was President Eisenhower's speechwriter and advisor?

A. Arthur Larson.

◆

Q. What 1929 graduate of West Allis High School choreographed such classics as "Carmen Jones" and Aaron Copeland's "Billy the Kid"?

A. Eugene Loring.

Q. What famous artist, known for his frontier paintings, spent much of the 1830s painting Wisconsin landscapes and portraits?

A. George Catlin.

Q. What Wisconsin abstract painter was the first American since Whistler to win the Grand Prize at the Venice biennale (in 1958)?

A. Mark Tobey, who grew up in Trempealeau.

Q. Where did Mississippi novelist Eudora Welty attend college?

A. UW-Madison.

Q. What best-selling novels did UW-Madison writing teacher Mari Sandoz write?

A. *Cheyenne Autumn* and *The Buffalo Hunters*.

Q. Where is the Lorado Taft sculpture "Recording Angel"?

A. Waupun.

Q. Who is the UW-Madison English professor and writer whose short-story collections include *Anagrams*, *Like Life*, and *Self-Help*?

A. Lorrie Moore.

Q. What 1925 book by historian Hjalmar Holand has sold more than 120,000 copies and has never been out of print?

A. *Old Peninsula Days* (about Door County).

Q. Who won a Pulitzer Prize in 1943 for his book *The Growth of American Thought*?

A. UW-Madison historian Merle Curti.

———◆———

Q. What Watertown resident became an advisor to Abraham Lincoln, Secretary of the Interior, and author of biographies of Henry Clay, Lincoln, and his own *Reminiscences*?

A. Carl Schurz.

———◆———

Q. What books of Wisconsin lore, anecdotes, and description did Fred Holmes write?

A. *Old World Wisconsin*, *Badger Saints and Sinners*, and *Alluring Wisconsin*.

———◆———

Q. What is the tallest building in Wisconsin?

A. Milwaukee's forty-two-story Firstar Center (601 feet).

———◆———

Q. What highway engineer wrote two historical novels about Wisconsin, *The Landlooker* (1958) and *Go Away Thunder* (1972)?

A. William Steuber.

———◆———

Q. What is the "Wisconsin" statue on the Capitol dome made of?

A. Bronze covered with gold leaf.

———◆———

Q. What UW-Madison English professor, poet, and novelist wrote *In the Wink of an Eye* and *My Life and Dr. Joyce Brothers*?

A. Kelly Cherry.

Q. When did Frank Lloyd Wright establish the Taliesin Fellowship for communal living and study of architecture?

A. 1932.

———————◆———————

Q. To what Madison bait dealer/philosopher does Madison writer George Vukelich turn for comments on life?

A. Steady Eddy.

———————◆———————

Q. When was the current Wisconsin Capitol built?

A. It was begun in 1906 and completed in 1917.

———————◆———————

Q. What was the 1944 sequel to *Caddie Woodlawn*?

A. *Magical Melons*.

———————◆———————

Q. How many Pulitzer Prizes did Madison native Thornton Wilder win?

A. Three (*The Bridge of San Luis Rey*, *Our Town*, and *The Skin of Our Teeth*).

———————◆———————

Q. What does the UW-Madison motto "Numen Lumen" mean?

A. God our light.

———————◆———————

Q. What sixty-year-old Frank Lloyd Wright design is finally going to be built in Madison?

A. The Monona Terrace Convention Center.

Q. What art museum is housed in a Tudor-style mansion built to become a museum after the owners' death?

A. The Paine Art Center in Oshkosh.

———◆———

Q. What type of decorative painting did Norwegian immigrants bring with them to Wisconsin?

A. Rosemaling.

———◆———

Q. What Milwaukee interior designer produced prairie style furnishings and murals for Frank Lloyd Wright?

A. George Niedecken.

———◆———

Q. What book did Frances Hamerstrom write about her experiences working with prairie chickens?

A. *Strictly for the Birds.*

———◆———

Q. What Spring Green theater performs only Shakespeare and other classics?

A. American Players Theater.

———◆———

Q. For what Scottish immigrant—a painter and poet who first lived in Milwaukee in the 1840s—is Durward's Glen named?

A. Bernard Isaac Durward.

———◆———

Q. What Shorewood High School graduate gained fame as one of the first female war correspondents?

A. Georgette Meyer ("Dickey") Chapelle (she covered World War II, the 1956 Hungarian uprising, and the 1959 Cuban revolution).

SPORTS & LEISURE

C H A P T E R   F I V E

Q. When did University of Wisconsin women's athletics achieve varsity recognition by the UW-Madison Athletic Board?

A. 1974.

Q. When did the three-point shot become legal in Wisconsin high school basketball?

A. The 1987–88 season.

Q. On September 9, 1992, what elite club did Robin Yount of the Milwaukee Brewers join?

A. Players with 3,000 career hits.

Q. What Wisconsin Badgers football player led the Big Ten Conference in passes defended against as a senior and was a first-round NFL draft pick in 1991?

A. Troy Vincent.

Q. What Madison woman won the first women's Olympic bicycle road race during the 1984 Olympics?

A. Connie Carpenter.

Q. Where was Ryne Duren, New York Yankee pitcher whose twenty saves topped the American League in 1958, born?

A. Cazenovia.

Q. Where did the University of Wisconsin Badgers play their last game of the 1993 regular season, to clinch a trip to the Rose Bowl?

A. Tokyo.

Q. Where did Pulitzer Prize-winning sportswriter "Red" Smith grow up?

A. Green Bay.

Q. Where was Badgers football great Elroy Hirsch born?

A. Wausau.

Q. What are Wisconsin's Division I college basketball teams?

A. Marquette, UW-Madison, UW-Milwaukee, and UW-Green Bay.

Q. What seven-foot-tall twins played on the UW-Madison men's basketball team in the early 1970s?

A. Kim and Kerry Hughes.

Q. What was the temperature on December 31, 1967, when the Packers defeated Dallas at Lambeau Field to earn a trip to Super Bowl I?

A. Minus 13 degrees (with a wind-chill factor of minus 48).

Q. Who was UW-Madison's first female All-American?

A. Track star and Olympic runner Cindy Bremser (1975).

Q. When were women first allowed to enter the Wisconsin state Golden Gloves boxing tournament?

A. 1994.

Q. Who was the coach at Marquette when they won the NCAA basketball championship in 1977?

A. Al McGuire.

Q. What famous Pittsburgh Steeler was born in Appleton in 1947?

A. Rocky Bleier.

Q. Where is John Heisman, for whom the Heisman Trophy is named, buried?

A. Forest Home Cemetery in Rhinelander.

Q. When did the Milwaukee Braves win the World Series?

A. 1957.

Q. What Badgers middle guard started forty-six consecutive games, was All-American in 1981, and went on to a brilliant pro career?

A. Tim Krumrie.

Q. Who did the Milwaukee Braves beat when they won their only World Series?

A. The New York Yankees (four games to three).

Q. What Wisconsin hockey player scored two of the four goals in the 1980 U.S. Olympic hockey team's defeat of the Russians?

A. Mark Johnson.

Q. In what year did the Brewers come to Milwaukee?

A. 1970.

Q. What was the fewest total points scored by both teams in a Wisconsin boys' high school basketball state championship game?

A. Fourteen (in 1925, when La Crosse beat Shawano 10–4).

Q. What former Brewer was named Most Valuable Player in the 1993 World Series?

A. Paul Molitor.

Q. Who is UW-Madison's all-time basketball scoring leader?

A. Robin Threat (1,901 points, 1989–93).

Q. What was the largest crowd ever to watch a football game at UW-Madison?

A. 80,024 (against Michigan in 1978).

Q. At what UW-Madison football game were more than ninety people injured when the crowd tried to rush the field at the end of the game?

A. The UW-University of Michigan game in 1993.

———◆———

Q. At what UW-Madison football game did the bleachers collapse, injuring hundreds of spectators?

A. The UW-University of Michigan game in 1902.

———◆———

Q. Why was Germantown resident Kevin Stenes named "ultra-marathoner of the year" for 1993?

A. He ran 164.2 miles in twenty-four hours.

Q. What major league team owns the Appleton Foxes?

A. The Kansas City Royals.

Q. Who coached the 1960 and 1963 Badgers Rose Bowl teams?

A. Milt Bruhn.

———◆———

Q. Where was top pro golfer Andy North born?

A. Thorp (in 1950).

———◆———

Q. What were the fewest total points ever scored in a Wisconsin boys' high school basketball state tournament?

A. Ten (in 1917, when Edgerton beat Galesville 7–3).

Q. When did the UW-Madison men's basketball team last win an NCAA basketball championship?

A. 1941.

Q. How much did the Milwaukee Brewers franchise cost the consortium of Milwaukee businessmen that purchased it?

A. $13.7 million.

Q. What NCAA national championships have been held at the UW-Madison Fieldhouse?

A. Boxing (1960) and women's volleyball (1993).

Q. Who gave Elroy Hirsch the nickname "Crazylegs"?

A. Sportswriter Francis Powers of the *Chicago Daily News*, in 1942.

Q. How many times have the Green Bay Packers played on "Monday Night Football" (as of the 1994–95 season)?

A. Twenty.

———◆———

Q. How long is the American Birkebeiner ski race?

A. Fifty-five kilometers (from Hayward to Cable, or sometimes vice versa).

———◆———

Q. Who was the last of Wisconsin's nine-letter winners, also star of the 1963 Rose Bowl?

A. Pat Richter.

Q. Where did Hank Aaron first play professional baseball?

A. Eau Claire.

———◆———

Q. What Badgers quarterback in the 1963 Rose Bowl was voted the game's Most Valuable Player?

A. Ron VanderKelen.

———◆———

Q. What Babe Ruth record did Hank Aaron break?

A. Most home runs in a career.

———◆———

Q. What were the Racine Belles, the Kenosha Comets, and the Milwaukee Chicks?

A. Teams in the All-American Girls Professional Baseball League.

———◆———

Q. Prior to 1993, when was the last time the UW Badgers football team won nine games in a season?

A. 1901 (when their record was 9–0).

———◆———

Q. What Milwaukee athlete won the women's wheelchair division in the Boston Marathon four consecutive years?

A. Jean Driscoll (1990–93).

———◆———

Q. How many major league records did Hank Aaron hold when he retired?

A. Five (pro games played, 3,298; RBIs, 2,297; plate appearances, 13,940; at-bats, 12,364; and home runs, 755).

Q. When did the Wisconsin Lottery begin?

A. 1988.

———◆———

Q. Who is the only American ever to win five gold medals in a winter Olympics?

A. Madison speedskater Eric Heiden (1980).

———◆———

Q. Who holds the National Football League record for most touchdown passes caught in a career?

A. Green Bay Packer Don Hutson (ninety-nine, 1935–45).

———◆———

Q. What team beat the favored Wisconsin Badgers in the 1984 Hall of Fame Bowl in Birmingham?

A. Kentucky (20–19).

———◆———

Q. What are all those people on the shore of Lake Michigan in Milwaukee and Sheboygan doing every year on January 1?

A. Swimming (they are members of the Polar Bear Club).

———◆———

Q. Who was Wisconsin's only Heisman Trophy winner?

A. Alan ("the Horse") Ameche (1954).

———◆———

Q. Who holds the UW Badgers' record for most yards gained in a football game?

A. Billy Marek (304 against Minnesota, November 23, 1974).

Q. Who holds the UW Badgers' record for most touchdown passes in a single football game?

A. Darrell Bevell (five, against Nevada, September 4, 1993).

———◆———

Q. Which Milwaukee Bucks are in the Naismith Memorial Basketball Hall of Fame?

A. Bob Lanier, Oscar Robertson, Dave Cowens, and Nate ("Tiny") Archibald.

———◆———

Q. Which player holds the National Football League record for most seasons leading the league in touchdowns?

A. Green Bay Packer Don Hutson (eight).

———◆———

Q. At what college besides UW-Madison did Elroy ("Crazylegs") Hirsch play football?

A. The University of Michigan.

———◆———

Q. Which UW Badgers football player holds the record for most rushing touchdowns in a single game?

A. Billy Marek (five, against Minnesota, November 23, 1974).

———◆———

Q. How many deer were killed during the record-setting 1991 Wisconsin gun deer hunting season?

A. 352,520.

———◆———

Q. What was the longest pass play in Wisconsin football history?

A. Eighty-nine yards (Tony Lowery to Lee DeRamus, against Eastern Michigan, September 28, 1991).

Q. What UW Badgers defensive back blocked a school-record three punts against Missouri in 1984?

A. Richard Johnson.

Q. Who holds the National Football League season record for average return yards on kickoffs?

A. Green Bay Packer Travis Williams (averaged 41.1 yards per return in 1967).

Q. Where did Joseph Linder, "the first great American-born hockey player," spend his final years, dying there in 1948?

A. Superior.

Q. Where did the UW Badgers play football before Camp Randall Stadium was purchased in 1893?

A. On a field at the end of State Street (now occupied by the State Historical Society, the Memorial Library, and the Library Mall).

Q. What famous early Badgers football player was known as the "Kangaroo Kicker"?

A. Pat O'Dae, who played in the late 1890s.

Q. When was the last time the Badgers played Marquette in football?

A. 1960.

Q. What National Football League player holds the record for most consecutive passes attempted without an interception?

A. Green Bay Packer Bart Starr (294).

Q. Where is the headquarters of the United States Curling Association?

A. Stevens Point.

—◆—

Q. Which was the only Big Ten team to beat the Badgers during the 1962 regular football season?

A. Ohio State (14–7).

—◆—

Q. Which team beat the Milwaukee Brewers in the 1982 World Series?

A. The St. Louis Cardinals.

—◆—

Q. What three Brewers hit more than thirty home runs during the 1982 season?

A. Ben Ogilvie (34), Gorman Thomas (39), and Cecil Cooper (32).

—◆—

Q. In what year did the Green Bay Packers join the National Football League?

A. 1921.

—◆—

Q. Who was the 1982 Cy Young Award winner?

A. Brewer pitcher Pete Vuckovich.

—◆—

Q. For what team was Jack Schneider playing in 1906 when he caught football's first legal forward pass?

A. Carroll College.

Q. In what year did the Brewers become the first major league baseball team to win a five-game championship series after losing the first two games?

A. 1982.

———◆———

Q. Who is the only major league baseball player to hit twenty or more home runs in twenty consecutive seasons?

A. Hank Aaron.

———◆———

Q. Who holds the Brewers' club record for hitting in most consecutive games?

A. Paul Molitor (thirty-nine, in 1987).

———◆———

Q. Who holds the National Football League record for the longest return of a fumble?

A. Oakland Raider Jack Tatum (104 yards for a touchdown against the Green Bay Packers, September 24, 1972).

———◆———

Q. What Boyceville-born outfielder played in the 1945 World Series with the Cubs, in the 1952 World Series with the Dodgers, and in the 1957 and 1958 World Series with the Braves?

A. Andy Pafko.

———◆———

Q. Who was the first American to win gold, silver, and bronze medals in speedskating, all in the same Olympics?

A. West Allis skater Sheila Young Ochowicz (1976).

———◆———

Q. Who is the only American ski jumper to win national championships in all four current classes?

A. Willis S. Olson of Eau Claire.

Q. When was the first Wisconsin girls' high school basketball state tournament?

A. 1976.

———◆———

Q. Where are Wisconsin's two official Indy Car racetracks?

A. West Allis (State Fair Park) and Elkhart Lake (Road America).

———◆———

Q. What Zenda resident skippered *America 3* in winning the 1992 America's Cup?

A. Buddy Melges.

———◆———

Q. What Brewers relief pitcher, now a Hall of Famer, won the 1981 Cy Young Award?

A. Rollie Fingers.

———◆———

Q. Which kicker holds the Super Bowl record for most field goals in a game?

A. Green Bay Packer Don Chandler (1968) shares the record— four—with San Francisco Forty Niner Ray Wersching (1982).

———◆———

Q. Why have graduating law students thrown canes over the crossbar of the goal posts before every UW-Madison home- coming football game since 1910?

A. Tradition says that they will win their first case if they catch their cane on its way down.

———◆———

Q. The Madison Muskies were a Class A franchise baseball team of what major league club?

A. The Oakland A's.

Q. When did the Braves move from Boston to Milwaukee?

A. 1953.

Q. Where was the first million-dollar gate in professional football?

A. In Green Bay (December 31, 1961).

Q. What was the nation's first high school athletic association?

A. The Wisconsin Interscholastic Athletic Association (formed in 1896).

Q. What team did the Green Bay Packers beat on December 31, 1961, to clinch the league championship?

A. The New York Giants (37–0).

Q. Where do the Beloit Brewers play their home games?

A. Harry C. Pohlman Field.

Q. For what Olympic sport do athletes train at the Pettit National Ice Center in West Allis?

A. Speedskating.

Q. Where was former major league baseball player, TV star, and radio announcer Bob Uecker born?

A. Milwaukee (1935).

Q. Which Milwaukee Braves player won the 1956 National League batting championship?

A. Hank Aaron (he batted .328).

———◆———

Q. When did UW-Madison first offer athletic scholarships to women?

A. 1975.

———◆———

Q. In what years did Madison's first professional baseball team, the Senators, play?

A. 1907 through 1914.

———◆———

Q. Where did Green Bay Packer legendary quarterback Bart Starr play college ball?

A. The University of Alabama.

———◆———

Q. What minor league baseball team played in Madison from 1940–42?

A. The Madison Blues (of the Class B Three-I League).

———◆———

Q. Where was the Brewers franchise before it came to Milwaukee?

A. Seattle (the Seattle Pilots became the Milwaukee Brewers).

———◆———

Q. What was the first Wisconsin-based professional baseball team?

A. Superior (of the Wisconsin-Minnesota League).

Q. In what year did the Milwaukee Braves lose the league championship to the Brooklyn Dodgers on the last day of the season?

A. 1956.

Q. How many cross-country skiers participate in the American Birkebeiner every year?

A. More than 6,000.

Q. Who are the Cheesemakers, the Marshmen, and the Hodags?

A. The high school teams of Monroe, Horicon, and Rhinelander, respectively.

Q. What record did West Allis speedskater Dan Jansen set in 1993?

A. He was the first to skate 500 meters in under thirty-six seconds (setting a world record of 35.92 seconds).

Q. What major league team owned the Class A Kenosha baseball club?

A. The Minnesota Twins.

Q. What was the first high school state champion recognized by the Wisconsin Interscholastic Athletic Association?

A. Milwaukee West High School (in track and field, 1897).

Q. What Milwaukee Braves pitcher won the Cy Young Award in 1957?

A. Warren Spahn (with a 21–11 record).

Q. What school won the first state high school basketball championship?

A. Fond du Lac (1905).

Q. The Milwaukee Braves won their second National League championship in what year?

A. 1958.

Q. What was the Braves' final season in Milwaukee?

A. 1965.

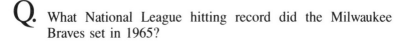

Q. When was the first franchise shift in the American League?

A. 1902 (the Milwaukee club moved to St. Louis).

Q. What National League hitting record did the Milwaukee Braves set in 1965?

A. Six players hit twenty or more home runs.

Q. Where was former Minnesota Vikings coach Bud Grant born?

A. Superior (1927).

Q. In what sport is Milwaukee resident Bonnie Blair an Olympic gold medal holder?

A. Speedskating.

Q. Where was star Philadelphia A's outfielder Al Simmons born?

A. Milwaukee (1902).

——————◆——————

Q. Who was the quarterback of tiny St. Mary's College in California in the early 1930s when they beat such football powers as USC, UCLA, and Alabama?

A. Marvin Miller of Kaukauna.

——————◆——————

Q. How many undefeated seasons have the UW football Badgers had?

A. Three (1901, 1906, and 1912).

——————◆——————

Q. Which Milwaukee Braves pitcher won the deciding game of the 1957 World Series?

A. Lou Burdette (shut out the New York Yankees, 5–0).

——————◆——————

Q. In their first season, 1968, who was the Milwaukee Bucks' leading scorer and only All-Star pick?

A. Jon McGlocklin.

——————◆——————

Q. What former Badger scored a seventy-nine-yard touchdown the first time he carried the ball for the Baltimore Colts?

A. Alan Ameche.

——————◆——————

Q. Who did the Milwaukee Brewers beat in the 1982 American League playoffs?

A. The California Angels (3–2).

Q. Where was the great New York Yankee shortstop Tony Kubek born?

A. Milwaukee (1936).

———◆———

Q. What series record did Brewer Paul Molitor set in the first game of the 1982 World Series?

A. Most hits in a game (five).

———◆———

Q. For what pro team did Elroy ("Crazylegs") Hirsch play after starring at Wisconsin?

A. The Chicago Rockets.

———◆———

Q. What Superior team won six national championships, three world championships, and a bronze medal in the 1992 Winter Olympics?

A. The Superior Curling Club.

———◆———

Q. Who won the 1958 World Series?

A. The New York Yankees (beat the Milwaukee Braves, 4–3).

———◆———

Q. Who was the American League's 1982 Most Valuable Player?

A. Milwaukee Brewer Robin Yount.

———◆———

Q. Where is the headquarters of the American Bowling Congress?

A. Greendale.

Q. What statistic made the 1965 Green Bay Packers-Dallas Cowboys football game unusual?

A. Both teams ended the game with minus yardage.

———◆———

Q. When did girls' high school athletic teams begin playing in state championships sanctioned by the WIAA?

A. During the 1970–71 school year.

———◆———

Q. Who holds the National Football League record for most points scored in a season?

A. Green Bay Packer Paul Hornung (176 in 1960).

———◆———

Q. Which team did the Green Bay Packers beat in Super Bowl I in 1967?

A. The Kansas City Chiefs (35–10).

———◆———

Q. What National Basketball Association player holds the record for most games played in his career?

A. Kareem Abdul-Jabbar (1,797 games: Milwaukee Bucks, 1969–75; Los Angeles Lakers, 1975–89).

———◆———

Q. What University of Wisconsin athlete won more NCAA track and field titles than any other woman in history?

A. Suzy Favor (nine).

———◆———

Q. Who won Super Bowl II in 1968?

A. The Green Bay Packers (beat the Oakland Raiders, 33–14).

Q. When did the UW-Madison football team win its first post-season bowl game?

A. 1982 (the Independence Bowl).

Q. What is the UW Badgers men's basketball team's single-game scoring record?

A. 120 points (beating Southern Methodist University, 120–82).

Q. Which Wisconsin high school has won the most boys' tennis championships?

A. Nicolet (twenty-one as of 1992).

Q. Who are the only two Milwaukee Brewers to hit home runs over the 482-foot center field fence at the old Polo Grounds in New York?

A. Joe Adcock and Hank Aaron.

Q. What was Curly Lambeau's football team before it was named the Packers?

A. The Indians (the team was sponsored by the Indian Packing Company).

Q. During the eleven years under Coach Vince Lombardi, how many league titles did the Packers win?

A. Five.

Q. When did the UW Badgers win their first NCAA Division I hockey championship?

A. 1973.

Q. Who were the UW Badgers' two All-American football players in 1981?

A. Tim Kumrie and Matt Vanden Boom.

Q. Which Milwaukee Braves player holds the club record for most home runs in a season?

A. Eddie Matthews (forty-seven in 1953).

Q. Where did Packer great Ray Nitschke play college ball?

A. At the University of Illinois.

Q. Who was the first UW-Madison woman athlete to win eight varsity letters?

A. Track star Suzy Favor (1987–90).

Q. How many NCAA hockey championships have the UW Badgers won?

A. Five (1973, 1977, 1981, 1983, and 1990).

Q. In what sport have the UW Badgers won the most national championships?

A. Boxing (eight).

Q. In which sport has UW-Madison produced the most Olympic athletes?

A. Rowing (fourteen).

Q. What former Milwaukee Brave holds the National League record for most career home runs by a pitcher?

A. Warren Spahn (thirty-five).

———◆———

Q. In what year did Vince Lombardi become coach of the Green Bay Packers?

A. 1959.

———◆———

Q. What three players were members of both the Milwaukee Braves and Milwaukee Brewers rosters?

A. Filipe Alou, Phil Roof, and Hank Aaron.

———◆———

Q. For what trophy do the University of Wisconsin and University of Minnesota football teams play?

A. The Paul Bunyan Axe.

———◆———

Q. What major league team owns the Class A Beloit baseball club?

A. The Milwaukee Brewers.

———◆———

Q. Who was the only University of Wisconsin quarterback to become an All-American?

A. Earl Girard (1944).

———◆———

Q. What University of Wisconsin female athlete qualified for three consecutive Olympics, earning a bronze and a gold medal?

A. Rower Carie Graves (1976, 1980, and 1984).

Q. What position did Wisconsin's legendary football star Alan Ameche play?

A. Fullback.

Q. Where was former Notre Dame and Green Bay Packers coach Dan Devine born?

A. Augusta.

Q. The numbers of what five Marquette University basketball stars have been retired?

A. Butch Lee (15), Dean Meminger (14), George Thompson (24), Don Kojis (44), and Bo Ellis (31).

Q. Which Wisconsin high school has won more boys' golf championships than any other school in the nation?

A. Madison West (fourteen as of 1992).

Q. What is UW-Madison's longest running football rivalry?

A. The University of Minnesota (since 1890).

Q. Who was the Green Bay Packers quarterback before Bart Starr took over that job?

A. Paul Hornung (Coach Vince Lombardi switched him to halfback).

Q. What was remarkable about the October 1982 football game between UW-Madison and Ohio State, played in Columbus, Ohio?

A. The Badgers won 6–0 at Ohio State, for the first time since 1918.

Q. Who was Bernie Brewer, a figure with a beer barrel for a body and a beer spigot for a nose?

A. The original Milwaukee Brewers logo.

Q. Who was named National Basketball Association's Rookie of the Year in 1970?

A. Lew Alcindor of the Milwaukee Bucks.

Q. What did angry fans do to show their displeasure with Green Bay Packers Coach Dan Devine?

A. They shot his dog.

Q. Who holds the UW-Madison record for most points scored in a single basketball game?

A. Ken Barnes (forty-two against Indiana in 1965).

Q. When was the last time the Marquette football team played in the Cotton Bowl?

A. 1937 (they lost to Texas Christian, 7–0).

Q. How many times have the Wisconsin Badgers played in the Rose Bowl?

A. Four (1953, 1960, 1963, and 1994).

Q. What famous name did a UW-Green Bay basketball star, a Green Bay Packer, and a singing star all share in the early 1990s?

A. Tony Bennett.

Q. What were the Milwaukee Bucks team colors before the 1993–94 season?

A. Forest green, red, and white.

———◆———

Q. Who was the only UW-Madison wrestler to win three NCAA championships?

A. Lee Kemp (1976, 1977, 1978).

———◆———

Q. Who holds the UW Badgers' regular season football record for most receiving yards in a season?

A. Lee DeRamus (920 in 1993).

———◆———

Q. According to the 1991 Survey of Hunting and Fishing, how many people in Wisconsin hunt?

A. 746,900.

———◆———

Q. Which quarterback holds the UW Badgers' football record for pass completion percentage in a season?

A. Darrell Bevell (68.8 percent in 1993).

———◆———

Q. Which Wisconsin player was named Most Outstanding Player in the 1973 NCAA hockey tournament?

A. Forward Dean Talafous.

———◆———

Q. In what activity did Milwaukeeans Bill Hackbarth, Paul Hess, and Craig York participate at the 1994 Winter Olympics in Norway?

A. Snow sculpting.

Q. What sports did UW-Madison eliminate in 1990 in an attempt to control athletic costs?

A. Baseball, men's and women's fencing, and gymnastics.

Q. Who was the first female president of the NCAA?

A. UW-Madison alumna Judith Sweet (1992).

Q. Who holds the UW Badgers' football record for most rushing yards gained in a regular season?

A. Brent Moss (1,479 in 1993).

Q. How did the Milwaukee Bucks get their name?

A. Through a contest that drew 14,000 entries.

Q. Who was named 1993 Big Ten Coach of the Year?

A. UW-Madison football coach Barry Alvarez.

Q. What Wisconsin player was named Most Outstanding Player in the 1981 NCAA hockey tournament?

A. Goalie Marc Behrend.

Q. In which two years did Madison golfer Andy North win the U.S. Open?

A. 1978 and 1985.

Q. In what league do the Milwaukee Admirals play?

A. The International Hockey League.

———◆———

Q. What is the largest margin of victory in a road game for the Wisconsin Badgers men's basketball team?

A. Thirty-six points (103–67 over Loyola Marymount in December 1993).

———◆———

Q. Where is the nation's first rails-to-trails biking and hiking trail?

A. The thirty-two-mile Elroy-Sparta Trail (opened in 1967).

———◆———

Q. Which Milwaukee Bucks player is one of only two NBA players to ever win back-to-back defensive Player of the Year awards?

A. Sidney Moncrief (1983 and 1984).

———◆———

Q. Where did Ron VanderKelen, who led the UW Badgers to a 1962 Big Ten football championship, play in high school?

A. Green Bay Preble.

———◆———

Q. When did the first women cheerleaders take to the football field at UW-Madison?

A. 1951.

———◆———

Q. Who are the eleven head coaches of the Green Bay Packers?

A. Curly Lambeau, Gene Ronzani, Lisle Blackbourn, Ray "Scooter" McLean, Vince Lombardi, Phil Bengtson, Dan Devine, Bart Starr, Forrest Gregg, Lindy Infante, and Steve Holmgren.

Q. Who was the quarterback of the 1960 UW Badgers Rose Bowl team?

A. Dale Hackbart.

Q. Who is the first UW-Milwaukee athlete to have her number retired?

A. Basketball star Jaci Clark (number 42).

Q. What Wisconsin high school wrestling team had the most female members?

A. The 1993–94 Bayfield-Washburn High School team (five).

Q. Where is Wisconsin's largest concentration of curlers?

A. Columbia County (five of the state's twenty-eight curling clubs).

Q. Who was the quarterback of UW's 1953 Rose Bowl team?

A. Jim Haluska.

Q. What is the longest winning streak in Wisconsin high school football?

A. Forty-eight games (by Manitowoc High School, before losing during the 1987 season).

Q. Who is the all-time leading scorer in Wisconsin high school girls' basketball?

A. Middleton's Angie Halbleib (2,378 points).

Q. Who is the all-time leading scorer in Wisconsin high school boys' basketball?

A. Wausaukee's Anthony Pieper (3,391 points).

Q. Who is the first Wisconsin high school track and field athlete to win titles in nine individual events?

A. Nekoosa's Heather Hyland (1993).

Q. Who is the winningest high school swimming coach in Wisconsin history?

A. Tom Hargraves, coach of Madison West, whose teams have won twenty state championships (thirteen boys' and seven girls') between 1977 and 1993.

Q. Who is the all-time leading scorer in Wisconsin high school girls' soccer?

A. Waunakee's Heather Willihnganz (150 points).

Q. When was football first made a sport at the University of Wisconsin?

A. 1889.

Q. Who coached the UW Badgers in the 1953 Rose Bowl?

A. Ivan Williamson.

Q. What Badgers sports team was the first to play in Japan?

A. The baseball team (toured Japan in 1909, playing nine games).

Q. What is Bucky Badger's full name?

A. Buckingham U. Badger.

Q. What is the only women's sport in which UW-Madison teams have won NCAA championships?

A. Cross country (1984 and 1985).

Q. Who was Curly Lambeau's college football coach?

A. Knute Rockne.

Q. What traditional English sport is played at Lake Park in Milwaukee?

A. Lawn bowling.

Q. In what years did Al McGuire coach basketball at Marquette?

A. 1964 through 1977.

Q. What former Minnesota Vikings Pro Bowl strong safety grew up in West Milwaukee?

A. Karl Kassulke.

Q. Who is the first National Football League player to catch 100 passes in two consecutive seasons?

A. Green Bay Packer Sterling Sharpe.

Q. What did Milwaukee athlete Dan Jansen finally accomplish in February 1994 after seven attempts?

A. He won an Olympic gold medal (1,000-meter speedskating).

———◆———

Q. In what sport did Madison native Sherri Steinhauer make $311,000 in 1993?

A. Professional golf.

———◆———

Q. According to a 1993 survey, which two Wisconsin cities have the highest percentage of residents who visit gambling casinos?

A. Green Bay and Appleton (forty-two percent in 1993).

———◆———

Q. Who represented Wisconsin on the 1994 U.S. Olympic hockey team?

A. Barry Richter (Madison) and Jon Hillebrandt (Cottage Grove).

———◆———

Q. Who was the only major league baseball player to play 1,000 games at shortstop and in the outfield?

A. Robin Yount (1,479 at shortstop and 1,113 in the outfield).

———◆———

Q. In what sport did Madison resident Marc McDowell win Athlete of the Year honors in 1992?

A. Professional bowling.

———◆———

Q. Who was the oldest player in the National Basketball Association?

A. Former Milwaukee Bucks player Kareem Abdul-Jabbar, at forty-two.

SCIENCE & NATURE

C H A P T E R   S I X

Q. What is Wisconsin's whitest Christmas on record?

A. 1950 (the entire state was covered with five to thirty-eight inches of snow, and it snowed all Christmas Day).

————◆————

Q. Where is Wisconsin's southernmost plot of boreal forest?

A. In the Ridges Sanctuary at Bailey's Harbor.

————◆————

Q. What did Stephen Babcock invent in 1890?

A. A simple test to determine the butterfat content of milk.

————◆————

Q. What geologic formations, usually associated with the southwestern United States, are found in central Wisconsin on the bed of glacial Lake Wisconsin?

A. Buttes and mesas.

————◆————

Q. What automotive breakthrough occurred in Clintonville in 1908?

A. Otto Zachow and William Besserdich developed the first successful four-wheel-drive automobile, the "Battleship."

Q. When did Wisconsin's first TB sanatorium begin operation?

A. 1903 (on the shore of Lake Nebagomon).

———◆———

Q. What breakthrough in electric power generation occurred at the Oneida Street Power Plant in Milwaukee in 1919?

A. Pulverized coal was first used as fuel for steam boilers.

———◆———

Q. Before Wisconsin became America's Dairyland, what crop dominated its agricultural production?

A. Wheat.

———◆———

Q. What is the minimum depth of the Mississippi River navigation channel?

A. Nine feet.

———◆———

Q. What Viroqua native is half of the first husband-and-wife astronaut team?

A. Mark C. Lee.

———◆———

Q. Which of the Wisconsin-born astronauts has flown the most space missions?

A. Watertown native Daniel Brandenstein (three on the space shuttle).

———◆———

Q. What is the Wisconsin state soil?

A. Antigo Silt Loam.

Q. What is special about the forty-inch telescope at Yerkes Observatory in Williams Bay?

A. It is the largest refracting telescope in the world.

Q. How many species of orchids are native to Wisconsin?

A. Twenty-three.

Q. Who buys the mussels harvested from Wisconsin's rivers?

A. The Japanese cultured pearl industry (pieces of the shells are used as "seeds" for pearls).

Q. When was the Oshkosh-based Experimental Aircraft Association founded?

A. 1953.

Q. Who was Woodruff's "doctor on snowshoes"?

A. Dr. Kate Pelham.

Q. What kind of geological formation is Rib Mountain?

A. A monadnock (rock that has not eroded as fast as its surrounding area).

Q. Why are guards posted along the Wolf River downstream from the Shawano Dam in late April?

A. To protect lake sturgeon as they spawn.

Q. How many types of soil are found in Wisconsin?

A. More than 500.

———◆———

Q. For what did UW professor Har Gobind Khorana win the 1968 Nobel Prize in physiology and medicine?

A. Work on the human genetic code.

———◆———

Q. What farming innovation did UW professor F. H. King produce in 1881?

A. The round silo (for storing cattle feed).

———◆———

Q. What species of fish was most common in the twenty-three million pounds of fish caught on Lake Michigan in 1880?

A. Whitefish (more than half the catch).

———◆———

Q. What varieties of cheese were developed in Wisconsin?

A. Colby and brick.

———◆———

Q. On average, what month is Wisconsin's warmest?

A. July.

———◆———

Q. What Wisconsin bird is among the oldest bird species on earth, having evolved more than twenty-five million years ago?

A. The common loon.

Q. Where was the granite for the sarcophagus for Grant's Tomb quarried?

A. Montello.

Q. For what is Wisconsin-grown tobacco used?

A. Cigars.

Q. Where is the nation's largest display of flowering crab apple trees?

A. Boerner Botanical Gardens in Milwaukee.

Q. What school was the first in the nation to offer a major in Scandinavian studies?

A. The University of Wisconsin (1875).

Q. What is the highest temperature ever recorded in Wisconsin?

A. 114 degrees (July 13, 1936, at Wisconsin Dells).

Q. Where was the first college major in psychology offered?

A. At UW-Madison (1888).

Q. When was Wisconsin's first heart transplant performed?

A. 1968.

Q. When did UW-Madison doctors perform the nation's first successful bone marrow transplant?

A. 1968.

Q. What is the lowest temperature ever recorded in Wisconsin?

A. Minus 54 degrees (January 24, 1922, at Danbury).

Q. How many farms are in Wisconsin?

A. 78,000 (as of 1993).

Q. What UW-Madison professors are known as the fathers of limnology?

A. Edward Birge and Chauncey Juday.

Q. Where was the nation's first college major in genetics offered?

A. UW-Madison (1910).

Q. What is the wingspan of an adult common loon?

A. Up to five feet.

———◆———

Q. When did the University of Wisconsin award its first PhD?

A. 1892 (to geologist Charles Van Hise).

Q. Where did air pioneer Charles Lindbergh attend college, accumulating an undistinguished academic record before dropping out?

A. UW-Madison (1920–22).

Q. What aquatic parasites devastated the Great Lakes commercial fishery in the late 1940s?

A. Sea lampreys (they came up the St. Lawrence River from the Atlantic Ocean).

Q. What is Wisconsin's mean annual temperature?

A. 43 degrees.

Q. What do volunteers for the Home Habitat Society do along Wisconsin roadsides?

A. Count roadkills.

Q. What Civil War artifacts were destroyed by Carthage College in 1993 after they sat in storage for more than 130 years?

A. A live cannonball, artillery shell, and shell fuses.

Q. What is the difference between white and yellow cheddar cheese?

A. Yellow cheddar is colored with annatto, a vegetable dye.

Q. How long is the average Wisconsin lake covered with ice during winter?

A. Four and one-half months.

Q. What is the only breed of dog developed in Wisconsin?

A. American Water Spaniel.

Q. How many books are in the UW-Madison library, the thirteenth largest university library in the nation?

A. Five million.

Q. What is the Wisconsin state fish?

A. The muskellunge.

Q. What federal laboratory in Madison, founded in 1910, looks for new uses for wood?

A. The Forest Products Laboratory.

Q. In 1909, what Wisconsin college offered the nation's first degree in agricultural economics?

A. UW-Madison.

Q. What was the subject of an article in Madison's *Progressive Magazine* that caused the federal government to take the magazine to court to try to prevent publication?

A. Instructions for building a hydrogen bomb.

Q. What nutritional discovery did UW professor E. V. McCollum make in 1913?

A. Vitamin A.

Q. In what Wisconsin county is farmland most costly?

A. Milwaukee (nearly $5,600 per acre).

———◆———

Q. Madison native John Bardeen was the first person to win what prestigious scientific prize twice?

A. The Nobel Prize for physics (1956 and 1972).

———◆———

Q. Who gives the winter reports on how deep the ground is frozen?

A. Gravediggers.

———◆———

Q. What Wisconsin county has the most dairy farms?

A. Marathon (1,400).

———◆———

Q. What endangered plant, found only in central Wisconsin, lives on what used to be the shore of glacial lakes?

A. Fassett's locoweed.

———◆———

Q. What is Wisconsin's number one cash crop?

A. Corn.

———◆———

Q. What international scientific prize did Stoughton native Parry Murphy share in 1934 for developing a treatment for pernicious anemia?

A. The Nobel Prize for medicine and physiology.

Q. What is the Wisconsin record muskellunge?

A. 69 pounds, 11 ounces.

—◆—

Q. For how long have UW-Madison students been making and selling dairy products (the famous Babcock ice cream)?

A. Since 1889.

—◆—

Q. How many Mississippi River locks and dams are in Wisconsin?

A. Five.

—◆—

Q. In what field of medical studies did Dr. William Beaumont conduct research at Fort Crawford in the 1820s?

A. Digestion (using a man whose gunshot wound to the stomach had healed improperly).

—◆—

Q. Where did Wisconsin's worst tornado strike, killing 117?

A. New Richmond.

—◆—

Q. What is the source of money for the Wisconsin Alumni Research Foundation (WARF)?

A. Patents on drugs and other discoveries made by UW-Madison scientists.

—◆—

Q. What is Wisconsin's average annual precipitation (rain and snow combined)?

A. 31.68 inches.

Q. What discovery did UW biochemist Karl Paul Link make in the late 1940s?

A. The anti-clotting agent dicumarol.

———◆———

Q. What southern Wisconsin lake is the most scientifically studied lake in the world?

A. Lake Mendota.

———◆———

Q. When did the last hog slaughtering operation in Wisconsin close its doors?

A. 1987 (the Cudahy plant).

———◆———

Q. On average, how many hours of fishing does it take to catch a legal muskellunge?

A. 100 hours.

———◆———

Q. Which UW-Madison scientist won the 1958 Nobel Prize for medicine?

A. Joshua Lederberg.

———◆———

Q. Of what fur product is Wisconsin the nation's top producer?

A. Mink pelts (900,000 annually, twenty-seven percent of the U.S. total).

———◆———

Q. Which UW-Madison researcher won the 1975 Nobel Prize in physiology-medicine for his research on viruses that cause cancer?

A. Howard Temin.

Q. When did the first Wisconsin mental hospital open its doors?

A. 1860.

———◆———

Q. On average, what is Wisconsin's coldest month?

A. January.

———◆———

Q. What discovery did UW researcher Conrad Elvehjem make in 1937?

A. He discovered that niacin prevents pellagra (a discovery that virtually ended outbreaks of the deadly disease).

———◆———

Q. How many Nobel Prizes have been awarded to UW-Madison faculty or alumni?

A. Twelve.

———◆———

Q. What did UW-Madison professor Harry Steenbock discover in 1924?

A. That vitamin D is produced by exposure to the sun's ultra-violet rays.

———◆———

Q. When did Wisconsin's first hospital open in Milwaukee?

A. 1848.

———◆———

Q. Patients with what maladies were barred from St. John's Infirmary, Wisconsin's first hospital?

A. Those with contagious diseases.

Q. In 1946, what Wisconsin community became the first in the state to add fluoride to its drinking water?

A. Sheboygan.

———◆———

Q. What are the three parts of Door County's Ridges Natural Landmark?

A. Ridges Sanctuary, Toft's Point, and Mud Lake Wildlife Area.

———◆———

Q. In August 1993, California replaced Wisconsin as the nation's number one producer of what agricultural product?

A. Milk.

———◆———

Q. What did UW-Madison professor Harold Rusch discover in 1941?

A. Which ultraviolet rays cause skin cancer.

———◆———

Q. What is the Wisconsin state domesticated animal?

A. The dairy cow.

———◆———

Q. When did the Door County apple and cherry growing industry begin?

A. 1858 (Swiss immigrant Joseph Zettel established the first commercial orchard).

———◆———

Q. What unique piece of equipment did UW Space Astronomy Lab scientists produce in 1968?

A. The Orbiting Astronomical Observatory, the first observatory in space.

Q. What is the Wisconsin state mineral?

A. Galena.

---◆---

Q. What medical breakthrough did UW-Madison surgeon Manucher Javid make in 1957?

A. A urea solution that alleviates swelling of brain tissues during brain surgery.

---◆---

Q. What is the Wisconsin state flower?

A. The wood violet.

---◆---

Q. What destroyed the resort business at Devil's Lake, allowing the state to purchase the area for a park?

A. Typhoid fever (contracted from contaminated lake water).

---◆---

Q. Where is the world's largest population of lake sturgeon?

A. Lake Winnebago and its tributaries.

---◆---

Q. What important screening test for newborn babies did UW medical school professor Harry Waisman make?

A. A test for phenylketonuria (PKU).

---◆---

Q. What Beloit native in 1922 found the first fossil dinosaur eggs in the Gobi Desert?

A. Roy Chapman Andrews.

Q. What Wisconsin watercourse is called "the hardest working river in the world"?

A. The Wisconsin River.

Q. Where in Wisconsin can you see the most bald eagles during the winter?

A. Along the Lower Wisconsin and Mississippi rivers (wherever there is open water).

Q. How many passenger pigeons were killed in central Wisconsin during the spring of 1871?

A. 1.2 million.

Q. How much of the nation's cheese did Wisconsin produce in 1919?

A. Two-thirds.

Q. What is Wisconsin's official symbol of peace?

A. The mourning dove.

Q. Who introduced alfalfa to Wisconsin as a feed crop for dairy cattle?

A. William Hoard.

Q. What did Racine resident William Horlick invent in 1876?

A. Malted milk (dry milk combined with malted wheat).

Q. What was Milwaukee's largest industry in 1880?

A. Meat packing.

Q. What nutritional discovery did UW researchers E. V. McCollum and Margaret Davis make in 1916?

A. Vitamin B.

Q. When did the worst tornado in Wisconsin history occur?

A. June 12, 1899.

Q. What is the Wisconsin state dog?

A. American Water Spaniel.

Q. When was the last passenger pigeon shot in Wisconsin?

A. 1899.

———◆———

Q. In 1930, what percentage of Wisconsin farms had electricity?

A. Eighteen percent.

———◆———

Q. In 1871, how many passenger pigeons nested in an 850-square-mile area of central Wisconsin?

A. 136 million.

Q. When nineteenth-century lumbermen first surveyed Wisconsin's northwoods, how much white pine did they estimate stood in the virgin forests?

A. 136 billion board feet (one-sixth of the nation's supply).

Q. How large is Horicon Marsh?

A. 31,653 acres.

Q. What is unique about UW-Madison's Biotron?

A. It is the only laboratory in the world that can simulate any environmental condition.

Q. What wetland crop is commercially harvested only in Wisconsin?

A. Sphagnum moss.

Q. What is the Wisconsin state rock?

A. Granite.

Q. What medical breakthrough did UW-Madison professor Folkert Belzer produce in 1987?

A. A new cold storage solution to preserve human organs for transplant.

Q. In 1866–67, Wisconsin led the nation in the production of what crop that is crucial to beer production?

A. Hops.

Q. How long has Gays Mills been producing prize apples?

A. Since 1905.

Q. When was Wisconsin's first state tree nursery founded?

A. 1911 (at Trout Lake).

Q. For what migration is Horicon Marsh internationally known?

A. The fall migration of Canada geese.

Q. Where is the state's monument to the passenger pigeon?

A. At Wyalusing State Park near Prairie du Chien.

Q. What did David Houston of Cambria patent in 1881?

A. The first roll film for cameras.

———◆———

Q. What is the Wisconsin state fossil?

A. Trilobite.

———◆———

Q. What were Wisconsin's three leading industries in 1910?

A. Lumber, foundries, and dairying.

Q. What Eagle River environmental education center was the first in the United States?

A. Trees for Tomorrow (founded in 1944).

Q. What Baraboo scientific research center is home to all fifteen species of cranes?

A. The International Crane Foundation.

Q. In 1993, how large was the average Wisconsin farm?

A. 219 acres.

Q. What pesticide, shown to cause difficulty in reproduction of falcons, eagles, and other birds of prey, was banned in Wisconsin in 1971?

A. DDT.

Q. Where was the Wisconsin record muskellunge caught?

A. The Chippewa Flowage.

Q. For what dance is crane expert George Archibald best known?

A. His mating dance with a whooping crane (to prepare the animal to breed).

Q. What endangered species has nested on the top of the Capitol building in Madison and on the Firstar Tower in Milwaukee?

A. Peregrine falcons.

Q. What is the Wisconsin state beverage?

A. Milk.

Q. Where is the oldest restored tall grass prairie in the world?

A. Curtis Prairie at the UW-Madison Arboretum.

Q. What is Milorganite?

A. Fertilizer made from Milwaukee's sewage sludge.

Q. What scientific course of study did Aldo Leopold develop?

A. Wildlife management.

Q. What link between a common food and cancer did UW-Madison researcher George Bryan find in 1969?

A. That artificial saccharine and cyclamates can cause cancer in lab animals.

Q. Where is the Leopold shack, where Aldo Leopold did much of his writing?

A. On the Wisconsin River in Sauk County, a few miles north of Baraboo.

Q. What intestinal parasite made hundreds of thousands of Milwaukeeans sick in April 1993?

A. Cryptosporidium.

Q. What pioneering dairyman (and Wisconsin governor) said "speak to a cow as you would a lady"?

A. William Hoard.

Q. What is the Wisconsin state wildlife animal?

A. White-tailed deer.

Q. What Wisconsin bird of prey can reach speeds of 200 mph while swooping down on its prey?

A. The peregrine falcon.

Q. What cancer-fighting drug did UW researchers V. Craig Jordan and Douglass Tormey discover?

A. The breast-cancer-fighting drug tamoxifen.

Q. What new papermaking technique did H. A. Frambach bring to Wisconsin in 1873?

A. A process that allowed paper to be made from wood pulp instead of rags.

Q. Of what industrial product was Wisconsin the nation's leading producer in 1914?

A. Large steam and gas engines.

Q. What did Whitewater science professor Warren Johnson invent in 1883?

A. The electric thermostat (which became the basis of Johnson Controls).

Q. What product did Racine businessman Samuel Johnson, creator of Johnson's Wax, sell before he developed his wax formula?

A. Wood parquet flooring.

◆

Q. When did the Kimberly-Clark Company introduce Kleenex?

A. 1924.

◆

Q. What Pewaukee printer is the largest privately held printing company in the United States?

A. Quad/Graphics.

◆

Q. When was Janesville's Parker Pen Company founded?

A. 1892.

◆

Q. How much sauerkraut do Wisconsin kraut processors produce annually?

A. 100 tons (making Wisconsin the nation's top producer).

◆

Q. What personal hygiene product became Kimberly-Clark's first big-selling consumer product in the years after World War I?

A. Kotex feminine napkins.

◆

Q. What Green Bay papermaker is the world leader in production of tissues made from recycled paper?

A. Fort Howard Corporation.

Q. What Wisconsin man founded the Sierra Club and is called "the father of the national park system"?

A. John Muir.

Q. What is the Wisconsin state bird?

A. The robin.

Q. What breakthrough in genetics did UW-Madison biochemist Gobind Khorana make in 1970?

A. Synthesizing a gene.

Q. What two environmentalists and authors worked for many years to restore populations of prairie chickens in central Wisconsin?

A. Frances and Frederick Hamerstrom.

Q. What does the Briggs and Stratton Company produce?

A. Small engines.

Q. What Wisconsin company began as a foundry in 1873 and became a leading producer of plumbing and bathroom fixtures?

A. The Kohler Company.

Q. What Milwaukee company, founded in 1903, is the nation's only producer of large motorcycles?

A. Harley-Davidson.

Q. What Chippewa Falls genius was responsible for creating many of the largest and fastest super-computers?

A. Seymour Cray.

◆

Q. What is the Wisconsin state animal?

A. The badger.

◆

Q. What company produced one of the nation's most popular mattresses in Kenosha from 1925 until 1962?

A. The Simmons Company (Beautyrest mattress).

◆

Q. What was the first product offered by the J. I. Case Company of Racine?

A. A horse-drawn thresher.

◆

Q. What did the Allis-Chalmers Company of Milwaukee produce?

A. Heavy machinery (including large engines, blast furnaces, sawmill equipment, and milling machinery).

◆

Q. What did the Simek family of Medford first produce at their tavern in 1962?

A. Tombstone Pizza.

◆

Q. What new treatment for immune deficiencies did UW professor Richard Hong develop in 1971?

A. A way to transplant cells from the thymus gland into children.

Q. What 1911 J. I. Case product changed the face of farming?

A. The first practical gas-powered tractor.

Q. What is the annual production of the Kikkoman Shoyu Company in Walworth?

A. Thirteen million gallons of soy sauce.

Q. What was Wisconsin's first public utility?

A. Milwaukee Gas Company (formed in 1852 to provide gas for public street lamps).

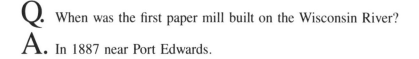

Q. What innovation in factory production did the A. O. Smith Company of Milwaukee pioneer in 1921?

A. The fully automated assembly line (used for production of car frames).

Q. What is the world's largest maker of lawn and garden tractors?

A. The John Deere Horicon Works.

Q. When was the first paper mill built on the Wisconsin River?

A. In 1887 near Port Edwards.

Q. How many states produce more cranberries than Wisconsin?

A. One (Massachusetts).

Q. What writing instrument was used to conclude World War II?

A. Parker Pens (used by both General Eisenhower and General MacArthur).

◆

Q. What is the Wisconsin state tree?

A. The sugar maple.

◆

Q. In what month does the average Wisconsin cow give the most milk?

A. May.

◆

Q. What percentage of the cheese in a product marked with the "REAL" seal is actually cheese?

A. 100 percent.

◆

Q. What game bird was introduced into Wisconsin by Capt. Frederick Pabst?

A. Pheasants.

◆

Q. What Wisconsin fish has changed the least since prehistoric times?

A. Lake sturgeon.

◆

Q. What killed Samson, the famous Milwaukee Zoo gorilla?

A. Heart failure.

Q. What was unique about the elm variety Sapporo Gold, introduced by UW-Madison plant pathologists in 1973?

A. It was the first artificially produced variety of elm that is resistant to Dutch elm disease.

———◆———

Q. What is the Wisconsin state insect?

A. The honeybee.

———◆———

Q. When did Wisconsin's first paper mill begin operation?

A. 1848 (in Milwaukee).

———◆———

Q. What breakthrough in contraception did Wisconsin Pharmaceutical Company of Jackson bring to the market?

A. The so-called "female condom."

———◆———

Q. What instruments did UW-Madison meteorologist Verner Soumi develop?

A. Instruments for satellites to measure radiation received, absorbed, and reflected from the earth and its atmosphere.

———◆———

Q. What discovery about fish migration did UW-Madison limnologist Arthur Hasler make?

A. That salmon imprint on the smell of their home stream and use smell to return to the stream for spawning.

———◆———

Q. What food is specifically exempted from Wisconsin's law protecting workers from hazardous substances in the workplace?

A. Lutefisk.

Q. Where did astronaut Deke Slayton grow up?

A. Sparta.

Q. What did Walworth County farmer John Appleby invent in 1878?

A. The twine binder (to bind sheaves of wheat mechanically).

Q. Where was North Central Airlines, precursor of Republic Airlines, founded in 1944?

A. Clintonville.

Q. According to a 1990 survey, how did UW-Madison rank among public institutions with graduates who are CEOs of Fortune 500 companies?

A. First.

Q. What Beloit businessman and inventor developed the first automobile speedometer?

A. Arthur Warner.

Q. What were Wisconsin's three largest industries in 1890?

A. Lumber, flour milling, and brewing.

Q. What did Grove Manufacturing, founded in Oshkosh in 1895, eventually change its name to?

A. Oshkosh B'Gosh.

Q. What Hartford company supplied custom luxury cars to the rich and famous of the 1910s and 1920s?

A. The Kissel Car Company.

———◆———

Q. When flour mills in the Fox River Valley closed in the late 1800s, what industry took over the mills?

A. Papermaking.

———◆———

Q. What is the Wisconsin state grain?

A. Corn.

———◆———

Q. When did Oscar Mayer expand its operations from Chicago to Madison?

A. 1919.

———◆———

Q. What did Wisconsin trapper Carl Eliason invent?

A. The snowmobile.

———◆———

Q. When did Austin Cofrin start the Fort Howard Paper Company?

A. 1919 (in Green Bay).

———◆———

Q. Who performed the world's first successful kidney removal operation in 1861?

A. Milwaukeean Dr. Erastus Wolcott.

Q. What was the first product Oshkosh B'Gosh sold?

A. Bib overalls.

Q. Who was the first female doctor admitted to a medical society in Wisconsin?

A. Dr. Laura Ross became a member of the Milwaukee County Medical Society in 1869 (six years after she first applied).

Q. Where did the world's first electric trolley operate, beginning in 1886?

A. Appleton.

Q. When did the first Chevrolets start to roll off the assembly line at the Janesville General Motors plant?

A. 1923.

Q. What edible product comes from the Wisconsin state tree?

A. Maple syrup.

Q. What did Daniel and George Van Brunt invent in Horicon in 1861?

A. The broadcast seeder for planting farm crops.

Q. Where are John Muir's mother and other family members buried?

A. Silver Lake Cemetery in Portage.